hobie

thanks for y
i hope you enjoy this
trip back in time

Tush

TURK

The Lives I've Lived

A Rebel *WITH* A Cause

Robert L. Tarozzi

The Lives I've Lived

The life and times of Robert 'Bob' 'Turk' 'Squeak' 'BobO' 'Fast-Bob' Tarozzi

Cover design by Richard Tarozzi
Interior design by Patricia Hamilton

Copyright © 2015 Robert L. Tarozzi

First Edition: December 2015

All rights reserved under International and Pan-American copyright conventionsw. No part of this book may be used or reproduced in any manner whatsoever without written permission from the author, except in the case of brief quotations embodied in critical articles or reviews.

ISBN: 978-1-943887-11-8

Published by
Park Place Publications
Pacific Grove, California
www.parkplacepublications.com

Printed in U.S.A.

PROLOGUE

*A cautionary tale that embodies Myth, Mad Schemes, Saga,
Fable, Folk and Fairy Tales, and some Truths.*

BELIEVE IT MY FRIEND, there was a time when individualism was a positive and meaningful pursuit. Unlike today where you must be part of a team and play by the rules, whatever that means. Thankfully I am from the former time and place. For all who missed that moment in time I will attempt to take you back where an individual was able to pursue a course to his liking, wear a multitude of hats and shift gears at a moments notice without losing momentum.

"Two or three persons having at different times intimated that if I would write an autobiography they would read it, when they got leisure, I yield at last to this frenzied public demand, and herewith tender my history."

— Mark Twain

**"Perhaps it seems to me
That I had several more
lives to live, and
could not spare any more
time for this one!"** —Thoreau

"If there's more, I want it." —A. Hart

"Imagination is more important than knowledge. For knowledge is limited to all we know and understand, while imagination embraces the entire world, and all there ever will be to know and understand."

— Albert Einstein

One of the great pleasures in life is doing what people say you cannot do!

Truly a Rebel WITH a cause.

THE NAME THAT FOLLOWED ME HOME

TURK: WHAT A STRANGE MONIKER for a pure bred Italian. I admit it does appear strange, on the surface, but it has a lengthy and convoluted history which I will share with you. Bear with me.

It all started in junior high school, in the wilds of Springfield, Massachusetts, probably sixth or seventh grade. Two of my buds were assisting me in conducting a particularly disruptive activity. Come to think about it, it was my very first venture into automotive testing—potato in the tailpipe. The buds where Billy King and Jimmy Olden. How the hell I remember those names I'll never know. Now I can't even remember where I left the damn keys. For what ever reason, one of them decided to dub me with the title 'Young Turk'. Why I'll never know, but he must have thought it fit. Over the years I have tried to research the term with only minimal success. The best I have come up with is the following: 'Young Turk: meaning a rebellious member of an institution, movement, or political party.' Rebellious I was, no question about it. The rest of the definition is probably hog wash because none of us were particularly versed in history, current events, politics, or anything that would produce that comprehensive of a definition. There you have it, but it ain't over!

We all moved on to different high schools and I lost the name tag. After graduating from Technical High School (note—Starting Q'Back and defensive linebacker for the 1954 Western Massachusetts Champions, sorry to drift) I joined the Strokers Hot Rod Club. At the first meeting I ended up sitting next to my junior high bud Jimmy Olden. He immediately proceeds to introduce me as the Turk—round two. That name stuck with me until after I graduated from college and moved to Detroit. But it ain't over!

I joined Chrysler Corp and attended their work/study program at the Chrysler Institute of Engineering. I fast tracked directly into the Race Group and snagged the project engineer job for the 1968 Hemi 'A' Body program. I designed the configuration, helped build it, and was the test driver for about six months. Immediately after the first test, we went into 'production' of 75 Plymouths and 75 Dodges at the Hurst facilities in Detroit. At one of the first drag meets for the 'production' vehicles I was strolling through the pits with the engineering boss Tom Hoover and the product planning czar Dick Maxwell. All of a sudden we all hear someone shout at the top their lungs "Hey Turk." Of course, I was the only one who turned around. Standing just behind us was Bill 'Farmer' Dismuke, chief tech inspector for NHRA. But known only to me; he had also been a member of the Strokers Hot Rod Club from Springfield, Massachusetts and an old friend.

After the introductions Bill said, "I hope I don't find any oxygen bottles in those Hemi cars!!" A little explain.

While a member of the Strokers, I owned a 1955 Ford Thunderbird and was constantly getting beaten by the local Corvettes. My devious mind, that had yet to be versed in the basics of engine design and performance, decided that the easiest way to supply air to the engine was to just supply the most essential component—oxygen. Why not?

I made a simple tubular fork, drilled it with holes, and mounted it on top of the carburettor. I then placed a small oxygen bottle on the driveshaft hump between the two seats. Attached a simple globe valve to the tank and ran a hose directly to the carburettor fork. Control, what control? Of course no electronics where available, simplicity was the way to go. I jetted the carburettor as rich as possible so that it would still 'run' without oxygen and just a little blipping of the throttle. I would sit at the starting line just keeping the engine running with manual control of the throttle. When the light went green I mashed the throttle and cracked on the oxygen. Sometimes when I shifted I backed off on the oxygen, but most of the time I regulated the oxygen by monitoring the spark knock. Hear the rattle, roll back the valve. It worked, for a while. I think I won a race or two, but black death reared its ugly head. Rings, pistons and cylinders became one. I do believe this was a one time event, but never-the-less old Bill remembered it well and my Chrysler cronies never let me forget my very first engine development program, and the moniker 'Turk'. But it ain't over!

Next, 1970, I moved from Detroit and landed in Southern California and the AAR Trans Am program. All was quite for a while. However in 1971 I was contracted to Chrysler to conduct their race engine development work at Keith Blacks in Southgate, California. Shortly after arriving at KB's Tom Hoover joined us to outline the program details. As soon as he walked in he greeted me with a gigantic, "Hello Turk," KB picked up on it immediately, and he stuck with it big time. During my stay at KB's I met many, many people from various areas of the racing/performance industry and the moniker continued to follow. But it ain't over!

The years drifted by and I involved myself in numerous mundane activities; it's a long way down from the top. Then one day the elder Turk had a vision, of Quixotic proportions, a modern steed on which he could go forth and do battle once again. Steel, aluminum, and various modern fibers of an exotic nature, powered of course by a four stroke reciprocating gasoline spark ignition engine, with but two wheels affixed to the earth. Yes, you guessed it, a modern-day motorcycle, with no less than 1000cc of wailing aggressiveness. Turk took to the track and became obsessed, once again, of being in control. To his surprise, and to others, the Turk was quick. Quick enough to be consistently nipping at the heels of much younger competitors. The moniker 'Fast Bob' became an addendum to Turk. I guess he's still evolving. But it ain't over!

To this day many people still bid the Turk a good day and good luck. And I must admit that after you follow my numerous adventures and misadventures you will see that my rebellious nature has never left, for good or bad, and always with cause. But it still ain't over!

Thanks Billy and Jimmy, I owe ya. And for you adventurous souls, please join me in my travels to a former time and place.

ACKNOWLEDGEMENTS

THIS WHOLE PAGE IS dedicated to my wife Elizabeth, without whom I would not be who I am and where I am today. We met when we were very young and it stuck. There is a song, circa 1950s, that was truly our theme song; "Too Young" by Nat King Cole

> *They try to tell us we're too young*
> *Too young to really be in love*
> *They say that love's a word*
> *A word we've only heard*
> *But can't begin to know the meaning of*
> *And yet we're not too young to know*
> *This love will last though years may go*
> *And then some day they may recall*
> *We were not too young at all*
> *And yet we're not too young to know*
> *This love will last though years may go*
> *And then some day they may recall*
> *We were not too young at all —Nunn & Bobby*

And here it is, almost, 65 years later. We've been sweethearts, lovers, parents, friends and buddies (a working companion with whom close cooperation is required). There it is; I said it and I mean it. Love you always.

And our kids, Bobby T and Kristine. Liz was the glue that held us all together. She did it all. She was a single parent before anyone invented the phrase. I wasn't a factor in my kids' lives until it was too late. I can only hope that they will read these pages, really read them, and perhaps they will come to understand not only what I did, but why I did it. Love you guys always.

CONTENTS

Prologue 3
The Name That Followed Me Home 5
Acknowledgments 9

1.	**The Formative Times**	15
2.	**The Nurturing Times**	21
3.	**The Beginning Chrysler Years**	33
4.	**NASCAR at Chrysler**	45
5.	**Drag Racing and NASCAR at Hurst**	55
6.	**Life at All American Racers**	61
7.	**Birth of the Keith Black Aluminum Hemi Block**	79
8.	**Oil Pans, Manifolds, Turbocharging .... and the Ax!**	87
9.	**Legal Detour**	99
10.	**I Hear the Roar Again**	105
11.	**Rest the Brain, Work the Body**	111
12.	**Bangladesh—Saving the World, Parte Uno**	121
13.	**Let's Go to Indy!**	125
14.	**Change Harley, Say What?**	131
15.	**What, Another Hemi Fuel Motor? You Got to Be Kidding Me!**	135
16.	**Back to Ventura and Harley D.**	139
17.	**A Little Diversion**	147
18.	**Engine Corporation Of America—Saving the World - Parte Due**	149
19.	**Hang On, One More Life—Motorcycles**	157

Epilogue 161
Tarrozi Photo Album 167

Part One

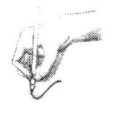

The Early Years

1 THE FORMATIVE TIMES

THE LIVES I'VE LIVED. The major direction of my life has always been automotive. My dream was to be a race car driver. It was never to be. Ah well. Man plans, God laughs.

I pray that you may never have,
The things you long for most,
The things we long for give to life,
The purpose and the gleam,
The things we get however fine,
Are never what they seem.
O' rather would I bid you keep,
A few small dreams in Trust,
Than see you have the things you want,
And watch them turn to rust. — Unknown

I'm not sure I truly believe this. I think if all my dreams came true, of all the things I wanted, I would continually polish them and cherish them. They may not be what they seem, but they're mine and I would never let them turn to rust! I believe that when you run out of dreams, you run out of life.

"A man is not old until regrets take the place of dreams." -John Barrymore

∞ ∞ ∞

IT WAS A SECRET PLACE—sort of. Dark and musty, no one else cared to enter, never mind hang around. I constructed it with care from the only materials available to me at the time, cardboard boxes. I spent very little time considering the details. The objective was to get it done and move on to the next phase, which, after all, was the real objective—or was it?

It was the first thing that I built with my very own hands. Little did I know that this project was to set in stone all of what I have done since. Get it done and move on, get it done and move on. I wish it were otherwise.

Perhaps I should have spent more time considering the spatial requirements, construction material, the construction process. In philosophical terms it would be the journey not the destination. But then again within a few days my secret place was a working darkroom, not bad for an eleven-year-old, twelve-year old, somewhere in there, kid.

My dad, Albert Joseph Tarozzi, I loved the man. He worked too much, he smoked too much, he drank too much, but he always had time. Time to listen, time to question, time to allow you to find the answer on your own, or at least he made you think so.

My dad was the hardest-working guy I ever knew. It seemed to me he never slept. He was always awake before me and he was always still hanging in there when I fell asleep.

Because he worked so much he was rarely home when I was. But he was always, and I mean always, available when I needed him.

He listened carefully and then suggested the things I might consider doing to solve my dilemma. I know now that we only talked when I had a dilemma. My fault, not his. Communication is a two-way process. But when you're young, the ability to listen seems to be missing from your make-up, at least it was in mine.

Children see different than adults.

My Mom, Albena Laura Carando Tarozzi. All I can say is that I was not her favorite. I had a younger sister, Joann, and younger brother, Richard. Little brother (LB) was the favorite, but it wasn't his fault. He was a little less trouble, I guess. I was so into myself and my dreams that I paid very little attention to anyone but myself. You see, I developed focus and commitment at a very early age. I had it for sure, but I didn't know what it was or were it would lead.

As a child I felt that most adults were limited in their thinking, stifling and crippling in their interactions with children.

All I ever wanted was to be able to think for myself, go in the direction I thought best and learn from my own mistakes. My father agreed, my mother did not. I don't know what my sister or brother thought, although they were probably too young to realize what I was and where I was headed.

I'm sure that parents think they know best. The fine line between guidance and dominance is difficult at best.

Children see different than adults.

AFTER HIGH SCHOOL I wanted to work in an endeavor that I loved and was extremely passionate about. My mother wanted me to go to college. I thought it was a waste of time. My dad understood, apparently, and bought me a mechanic's toolbox and got me a job at the Ford dealership through one of his friends.

Life went well; I got married, worked during the day at the dealership and worked at night on race cars, motorcycles, et cetera.

THE OTHER SIDE

BUT BEFORE YOU COME to the conclusion that I was walking around with a halo around my head, I need to show you the other side. This other side lives in every child. Parents beware and hope for the best. My high school was about three miles from my house. I had two other buddies who would walk to school with me. We would cut through the woods and over dale in an attempt to make a straight line out of the walk. Somewhere before we reached the high school we would pass through the railroad yard. When the trains passed though the yard they would be moving very slowly. We started by doing the usual tricks like placing pennies on the track and flatten them out to the size of quarters. Occasionally, some nitwit, dumber than us, would flush the toilet as they passed us. I do believe that it was intentional. Not funny.

Then we graduated to grabbing the ladder, known as the sill steps, ride along for a few feet, then jump back down. Great fun. Then one day someone, I know not whom, got the brilliant idea of climbing up to the top of a freight car and view the sights. So we did. By the time we all reached the top of a car the train began to pick up speed and jumping off did not seem very appealing. I don't know what the other guys were thinking but my analytical brain was already at work. I was not sure, but I hoped that the train would slow for a curve before we got going too fast. Right on the mark. As we approached the Smith & Wesson plant just north of the city, the train slowed down. I didn't know why, and didn't ask. Apparently the other guys had come to the same conclusion and we were down the sill steps in a New York minute. Solid ground was a welcome sight. The walk to school that day was a little longer than usual, and I don't think we hopped any trains after that. We were dumb, but not stupid.

Children see different than adults.

ANOTHER OFF-THE-DEEP-END adventure was seeded in a gyrocopter escapade. A gyrocopter is a type of aircraft that uses an unpowered rotor to develop lift and an engine-powered propeller to provide thrust or forward motion.

A very good friend of mine, Bob 'Wimpy' Lynch, had purchased a gyrocopter kit and asked (conned) me into helping him to assemble and build the basic structure. Initially the plan was to build the main structure without the engine and we would tow the unit to test the lift and airworthiness capabilities. Again man (boy) plans and God laughs. Big time.

During construction, the decision was made to build the propeller from scratch instead of purchasing a ready-made prop. You see it coming, don't you? We attached the completed gyrocopter with a long and sturdy rope to my trusty '39 Ford four-door convertible, top down, of course. Down the road we went. In our infinite wisdom we didn't choose a deserted roadway, void of obstacles and folks. We just drove down the street from Wimpy's 'hangar'. With Wimpy at the controls of the 'copter, we got up a little speed and, lo and behold we achieved lift! Up into the trees it rose, an awesome sight to see. Then I heard a crack, or was it laughter? The propeller had succumbed under the strain and the remaining craft plummeted to the ground and was seriously wounded. The pilot, Wimpy Lynch, was unscratched. We assessed the damage and decided that it was time to move on to other adventures. This time we made a good decision.

Children see different than adults.

My life was in constant motion and I had a passion for designing and building cars and motorcycles. However, I began to realize the limitations of a high school education especially when I had only attended classes two or three days a week. Nevertheless, I knew now I must go to college. The family money tree was bare. When I turned down the chance to go to college after high school, my brother stepped in and picked up the cash. He put it to good use. It seemed that he was going to become a professional student while I was emerging myself in grease and grime. Everything for a purpose. Even though life was hard, college was easy, relatively speaking. I graduated magna cum laude, second in my class. Went on to get a masters degree in automotive engineering and pursue the windmills of racing, whatever and wherever they were.

∞ ∞ ∞

I am now an adult but will always look at the world through the eyes of a child.

2 THE NURTURING TIMES

For this mythical tale I shall first take you through my early experiences, where at some point I came to a definitive fork in the road, which I chose not to take. I'll never know why.

Defining moment. Whenever I think about how it all began, the year 1952 and *Hot Rod* magazine comes to mind. I was just a lad of 14 or 15 reading an issue of *Hot Rod* magazine. I don't know why I chose that magazine, but I was reading it cover to cover, totally engrossed. I came to an engine buildup article and I clearly remember studying a photograph of the front of the engine. The caption mentioned the camshaft and crankshaft and it appeared that they both rotated in some fashion. But for the life of me, I couldn't figure out their relationship or what the difference was, if any. I asked my dad, but he didn't know either.

The quest began, the game was afoot!

I decided—make that needed—to get my hands dirty. Any piece of machinery or gadget would do. Take it apart, put it back together. That was my mantra, although at that time in my life I didn't have a clue as to what a mantra was. Words were never my thing.

It started like with most teens of the 50s -- CARS. Start small and then work up. My dad's cars were handy so I started there. Fix something small, break it, repair it, and move on. Progress! At 15 my first vehicle purchase was a 1939 Ford four-door convertible -- cool was the word. It was soon apparent that it needed a 'little' work -- parts were tough to come by so I bought a second one—why not? If one is good two is better! A little rubbing, kicking and banging and it was up and running. Wait a minute—I'm only 15, holy sh*t now what? I continued to polish, take it apart and put it back together again (one more round).

License time, coming up on 16, but my birthday was the 22nd of December and the DMV would be closed for Christmas. Now if I waited until I was actually 16, too late, I'd have to wait a week. Devious plotting told me that I could show up on the 20th or 21st and make an appointment, never mind that I'm still only 15, just stand tall. I got the appointment, passed the test, was there ever any doubt?— and haven't stopped yet!

From there I built various cars for myself and cars and engines for my friends. Hot rods, coupes and roadsters, numerous Chevy powered 'street' vehicles, a 1932 coupe with an Oldsmobile engine. Later this engine was transplanted into a rear engine roadster. One especially memorable 'racer' was a 1956 Austin Healey that shouldered numerous superchargers throughout its fabled life: McCulloch, Latham and a GMC 6-71. Unfortunately turbos were virtually nonexistent so one never made it under the hood. A Chevy powered roadster build strictly for dragracing. A Chevy powered '38 Chevy short-track stock car. Motorcycles were amassed from various baskets of parts. I raced them at drag races, 'roundy rounds' and an occasional motorcycle scrambles or hill-climb. It was just nuts, bolts and grease everywhere. It was the dealership by day and the backyard garages by night. I just had one tool box so I would move it with me in the trunk of my car—until it got too heavy to lift.

Somewhere along the line I joined the Strokers Hot Rod Club. Just a bunch of rag tag guys whose main purpose in life was to do what others said they couldn't do, and do it well. I was technically astute but financially devoid of monetary wherewithal, a.k.a., a poor boy. But this didn't stop me from being in the middle of it all. I would just show up with tools and skill in hand.

The crew: Jerry Lavoie, Tom Shea, Ed Ruggeri, Ed McGrady, Roger Walling, Bob Zepke, Carl Debein, Donny Allen, Felix Valetti, Don Witcowski, Xenophon Beak, Johnny Nye, Bill 'Farmer' Dismuke, Tommy Fisher, Bobby Shelb, Bob Casey, et al.

These were the principal guys that I remember; forgive me, those of you I have forgotten, all of whom were diehards, dedicated to racing—period. Be it street or track, it was truly in our blood and as far as I can remember most stayed true to form. A few have passed on as I write this tome, brief as it is. A few went on to greater fame and a few hopefully on to fortune.

The most elevated personality was Bill 'Farmer' Dismuke. He rocketed up the charts to become the high priest of NHRA drag racing tech. He was The Man. We would meet again under amazingly different circumstances, circa 1968.

Before I leave this spot in time I would like to give you one version of the true meaning of dedication and commitment. Picture this, if you can. A couple of guys pushing a brandy-new '57 Chevy convertible—by hand, mind you—down the street though traffic, hood off, engine and tranny nowhere to be seen. Not a single payment had been made. You might say that we were not exactly the brightness bulbs in the package.

Two days earlier:

Somehow I ended up with a channeled '32 roaster in my garage/shop, a roller, as it were. The details are not clear, but I do believe that the vehicle was 'dropped' off by Don Witcowski, member in good standing of the Strokers. I also believe that he must have donated the car because he never attended any of the drag meets that ensued, and I'm sure I didn't have the funds to buy it. The other member of the gang was Ed McGrady, proud owner of a brandy-new Chevy convertible complete with a high output 283 V8 with fuel injection, temporarily.

On this fateful night we decided the mighty Chevy V8 would be better served by being installed in the 32 roadster. Without further delay we extracted the engine and trans and forthwith rolled a powerless body-in-black down the street to Ed's house. His dad was standing on the front porch. He didn't say a word, just shook his head, turned around and went inside the house. He was a quiet guy. We did assure him that the convertible would receive a transplant before the week was out.

It was more like three weeks and the 'replacement' was a junkyard 265 with a sweet four barrel carburettor–ran smooth as glass. But that's not the end of this tale.

After completing the roadster and 'rebuilding' the convertible, we were headed to the dragstrip, once we got a trailer. None of the drag guys had trailers yet so we borrowed one from a local round track racer. Pure evil, the trailer, not the racer. We loaded it up and were ready to roll a little after midnight. I was slowly motoring out of my long driveway when my dad came home. He had just closed down his restaurant for the night. He came over to our rig and examined it with a cautious eye. In his younger days he had been a truck driver for a produce company. He spotted the unattached chain and immediately cautioned us as to the necessity of having it properly attached between the car and trailer. We objected, of course we knew better, but in the end we attached it as instructed and off we went. I believe there were four of us: Eddie was at the wheel of his refurbished Chevy, Felix Valleti in the center front and yours truly in the passenger's seat—no seatbelts, of course. Good old Roger Walling had commandeered the back seat so that he could sack out.

We hit the turnpike and headed east. We were destined for Maine. We didn't get very far, perhaps ten miles down the pike, and the trailer was a weaving. The Massachusetts Turnpike is a wide four-laner with an extra wide V-shaped grass and dirt divider, ultimately our savior. Gradually the trailer's weaving began to increase and we were losing the wheels one at a time. Eventually all four wheels were ripped off and tossed aside, trailer with roadster dragging on the ground. Ed said he couldn't hold on any longer and we were headed for the center divider strip. The car tunneled into the soft center divider, and here's the good part: the car rolled only once. The trailer acted as an anchor, secured by the chain, and we were brought to an abrupt stop.

Ed and Felix got tossed out of the drivers door; Roger was fast asleep in the back and didn't have a clue as to what had happened except that his siesta was disturbed. I, on the other hand, was missing in action. Ed, Felix and Roger were all running around yelling "Turk, Turk where are you?"

It wasn't too long before they located me, stuffed under the dash, out cold. They hauled me out and my first words were, "Where the f**k is my tool box?".

Little explain here. Before we left, I loaded my precious toolbox into the open rear section of the roadster, behind the driver's bucket seat. After regaining some small margin of consciousness, I assumed the whole rig had rolled over and my toolbox was scattered to the winds, perhaps along miles of turnpike. As it turned out the trailer/roadster was still upright and my toolbox had not suffered any trauma.

The Chevy convertible, on the other hand, was a total, total. The top was completely flattened and was resting on top of the door belt-line, and I mean completely flattened. When we saw the car the next day nobody, but nobody, could believe that anybody had lived through that performance. Injuries—one minor cut to the head, five stitches, to the unfortunate Turk. That taught me to never sleep under the dash again.

Summary and conclusion: My dad saved our asses with his insistence on attaching the chain between the car and the trailer. Without the chain and the trailer as an anchor, the tow car would have continued to roll and probably crushed everybody.

Looking back now, I can see that this was the first of many saves that my anonymous guardian angel would be forced to put into play. I was a risk-taker, it was in my genes. As I use to tell anybody who would listen, I was a Doer, not a 'Didder'. Fortunately I also had a survival gene which I would call upon many, many, times in the future.

In a sense I owe a lot to these guys, this old gang of mine. They got me started. Once I got the ball I carried it a long, long way. Thanks guys, I'll never forget ya!

BTW for anyone interested in more details of the Strokers and all the other early hot rod clubs in New England, I highly recommend the well-researched book by A. B. Shuman entitled Cool Cars, Square Roll Bars. Those were the days!

MOVING ON

LIFE WAS MOVING ON, never a lull in the activities, but something was missing. And then a sliver of reality set in. Rational Thinking 101.

Okay, I read all the magazines and books and built all the cars and engines just like the pictures. But that only got me to where they were. How to get ahead of the curve was the big question. Never being a stalwart scholar in high school, the obvious took a while to become apparent. The solution was college. I tried initially to circumvent the process. I procured several college-level workbooks on the subject of machine design, never mind the preliminaries, get right to the core. Whoa, I didn't have a clue. It might as well have been written in Greek. As a matter of fact it was! Sigma, beta, epsilon, summations signs, more symbols then numbers. What the hell was this crap, what did it mean, and what did it have to do with building race cars?

Everything!

Before actually going to college I busied myself with various activities. Worked day and night on cars, raced the cars whenever I could, and oh, by the way, I got married. Not more than a few months into wedlock, I took off for California—to find myself, I guess. Ever faithful Liz hung in there, even though she was pregnant. (What an asshole I was—still?) When I 'found' myself, don't believe it, I returned to the Right Coast to continue the search. A defining, Divine Moment took over the search and pushed me ever closer to the ultimate shaping of my mind and goals.

Upon returning to reality, this prodigal son was desperately seeking a direction.

THE BEGINNING PATH

MY PASSION FOR DESIGNING, building and driving cars and motorcycles was a given. I do believe it was programmed into my genetic makeup. But I have often wondered what the major event was that moved me in the direction that would ultimately mold my character and creative instincts. Was this blossoming by chance or intent? If I had to pick one event or influence, it would probably be my time at Worthington Pump in Holyoke, Massachusetts.

I had enrolled at Western New England College in my hometown of Springfield, Massachusetts. I started in the night school, later switched to the day program. By going to school nights I was able to continue to work as a mechanic, machinist, whatever.

I must have been 19 or 20, I can't remember, but somehow I landed a job at Worthington Pump. I'm not sure what I was hired as, something along the lines of engineering apprentice. No degree, you see. I was still in college, bouncing back-and-forth between evening and day classes.

I do remember it was wintertime, cold and snowing. The lab was testing their four-stage high-pressure air compressor that was enclosed in a doghouse-like structure, complete with heaters, stage unloaders and operating ventilation shutters. The unit was being run 24/7 out in the alley in order to be exposed to the elements. The lab techs would have to go out into the alley, turn on the recorder and read the data off the recorder that was attached to the unit. I believe they skipped the night shift collection. I suggested we automate the process so they could collect the data on a 24-hour cycle.

Remember, this was the mid-60s; no wireless electronic gismos were available. I had spotted an old school classroom schedule clock mounted on the wall in the lab somewhere. Originally the school schedule bells would be controlled by a paper tape punched with holes. You see where I'm going here! Sure enough, I 'programmed' the tape to open and close a circuit every hour and connected this circuit to a brush recorder. Action without human intervention. I was declared a genius. Edison would've been proud. Now, what if I made a printed circuit board? No, just kidding.

In the meantime, under the cover of darkness, I was researching the possibility of getting a masters degree in a work/study program with one of the major manufacturers in Detroit. And of course, it goes without saying there was racing floating around in that concoction of my thoughts and dreams. In the 60s the factory racing programs were moving and shaking and I planned on being there.

For the next month or so I did various jobs in the laboratory and then one day the chief engineer called me into his office. He apparently had the feeling that I was an 'electrical genius' because of my accomplishments, so to speak, in the lab. The current situation was that they needed to completely instrument one of the doghouses with a functioning control and readout panel. They also needed somebody to design the panel and all the electrics that were required, and then layout the circuitry. Of course I could do that, says I. So I began ordering parts and pieces and laying out the circuitry in an orderly fashion in a layout drawing. When this was done I handed them over to the boss man and he passed it on to the lab guys; lo and behold they panicked. There was nobody in the lab that could actually do the wiring. Either they couldn't or didn't want to, or were scared of failure, I don't know, but there it was—gridlock.

At this point I was elected to 'transfer' to the lab and proceed with the wiring process. It wasn't easy, but I had a hedge: I had 'invented it,' and I had wired a shop or two in my short life to-date. I nailed together a wiring layout board on a piece of 4x8 plywood, thinking ahead to the production of these beauties. In a couple of weeks I had the circuit wired and installed in the doghouse.

The bosses descended from unknown orifices and portals into the unpretentiousness of the laboratory. The pressure was on, pun intended. The button was pressed and the unit fired up. The heaters heated and the ventilation shutters flapped in the breeze, but, oh no, the unloaders didn't unload. The mighty Casey had struck out. But he, I, was not defeated. After the lab was cleared of the big guns I autopsied the corpse, alone I might add. Cut to the chase, one of the relays that controlled the unloaders was defective. It was replaced and the doghouse and all its dependents were up and running. I was redeemed in the eyes of my direct boss, but I know not of the upper level chieftains.

I'm sure I was headed for bigger and better things, but, a big but, I had bigger and better goals in mind. I had been accepted to the Chrysler Institute of Engineering in Detroit.

At the time I didn't give a second thought about leaving Worthington, or to the accomplishments I had achieved or to the effect it would have on my future. And it wasn't until now, as I reflect back on the whys and wherefores, that I can appreciate the significance of my time there.

Now that I am looking back, hindsight is an awesome tool—the ability to understand the question after you have the answer. In my experiences at Worthington, and in all my future undertakings, I did things I had no experience or knowledge for doing, but managed to pull them off with amazing success. I know this sounds egotistical and boastful, but as you proceed through this cautionary tale you will see that I have done and succeeded at things I had never done before.

As I stated, I had no previous experience or knowledge of what I was about to pursue, but damn it, I was moving down the road at 100 mph hell bent for the finish line, wherever the hell it was. I imaged things, mostly solutions. If I needed to design a widget (whatever the hell a widget is) I would go inside the widget, in my mind, of course. I would imagine what it needed to become whole and just do it. That's about as cornball as you can get, but I believe it and I hope, as you read through these mythical tales, you will become a believer as well.

Albert Einstein said it best. "Imagination is more important than knowledge. For knowledge is limited to all we now know and understand, while imagination embraces the entire world." He probably meant the universe.

I see knowledge, especially the book learning portion, as just lumps of coal. Lots of potential, but no heat, no flame. Imagination is the flame of accomplishment. OK, coal is needed to generate a flame, but there are many other ingredients that can generate a flame. So aren't there many ingredients that can flame the imagination, knowledge aside?

OK enough of this self-serving, soft-soap crap. Lets get on to the narrative of big time racing as it was in the 60s and 70s, 1960s and 1970s, that is. The future is waiting to happen.

> ***Perhaps it seems to me***
> ***That I had several more***
> ***lives to live, and***
> ***could not spare any more***
> ***time for this one!*** *—Thoreau*

Amen to that! Let's get started.

Part Two

The Automotive Years

3 THE BEGINNING CHRYSLER YEARS

Bob Tarozzi, that's me, worked for Chrysler Corporation from 1965 to 1969 as a Project Engineer in the Special Vehicles Group (read: Race Group). I did a stint at Hurst, of shifter fame. I was later contracted, through AAR, as a designer and race car engineer for the 1970 Trans Am Barracuda. Between 1971 and 1980, I was contracted to Chrysler to do all their race engine development work at Keith Black Racing Engines in Southern California. Etc, etc.

B.C. (BEFORE CHRYSLER)

Just to refresh your memory, I started building cars at 14 and raced cars at 16. College wasn't in the cards when I graduated high school, so I got a job as a mechanic and then trained to become a machinist. I have always subscribed to Mark Twain's insights into the real world: "Don't let schooling get in the way of your education." Amen. I got married and was making a lot of money as a line mechanic in various dealerships. I'd get paid the flat rate, but I could beat the book by half. When I accepted the fact that school was the only way to get ahead and find a job with a car company in Detroit, I enrolled at Western New England College in my home town of Springfield, Massachusetts.

I graduated with a BS in Mechanical Engineering, magna cum laude, in 1965. I looked at GM. They had a five-year undergrad program, but they wouldn't allow me to transfer credits from my four years of college, I would have to start from scratch. Ford had nothing. Chrysler had a two-year program leading to a master's degree in automobile engineering. Chrysler flew me to Detroit to attend a two-year work and school program.

The first week at Chrysler was an orientation class. They put up a big display board with all the departments where jobs were available. It was a rotation program working three-to-four months in one job before rotating to the next. You took five rotations in the two-year program.

LEARNING THE ROPES

THE ORIENTATION GUY POINTED to a flag at the bottom of the chart and said, "That's the Special Vehicles Group. Don't any of you ask me about this group because this is the race group and you guys can't go there."

Damn! That's what I wanted to do. I'm usually not a forward-type person, but I looked in the company phone book and found the department head of Special Vehicles, H.P. Bruns, the chief engineer. There were four-to-five people in that group: Tom Hoover (Drag Racing), Larry Rathgab (NASCAR), Jim Thornton and Pete Hutchinson, as well as Dick Maxwell in Product Planning)

I called H.P. and it turned out I had more race car experience than any one of the other guys there with regard to building, tuning and chassis set-up. At this time, my soul was into suspension design. I pitched all the angles to H.P. to get into the department, but no luck. Then, an inspiration! I told him it wouldn't cost him a dime to hire me because the Chrysler Institute paid my salary.

A pause, then, "Deal!"

INSIDE THE RACE GROUP

AT SPECIAL VEHICLES, I was assigned to Tom Hoover. Theoretically, the Special Vehicles Group had a budget in every department within the corporation for their projects. However, it was one thing to have the budget, another thing to have the manpower. If Bruns were to have a meeting with the chief engineer of the brake department and say we want to develop a disc brake for NASCAR, which they were trying to do at the time, oh well, we've got the money but we don't have any manpower.

I was quick to learn who the dedicated (enthusiastic) guys were in all these departments, and I would go to them. They would accomplish more on their lunch hour for me than if I walked in the front door and went by the book. We, the Race Group, were known as the Turks in the company because we got things done. Most people didn't like the Turks because they interrupted the work flow. Most managers, but not all, didn't care for my backdoor approach but let it slide. I had no official title when I did this, except perhaps 'asshole.' And as far as I could tell, it was accepted, and appreciated by the powers in the Race Group. Once I established all those contacts I was the group's golden boy. Usually, those enthusiasts were the best guys in their departments, and they enjoyed doing the race stuff more than their regular jobs.

I went through two or three rotations (out of the five), and Pete Hutchinson, whose grandaddy previously had been Chief of Finance for Chrysler Corp, left the group and went to work for Car and Driver magazine (that was before Pat Bedard came aboard the magazine). Pete's job was open and I wanted it. I had rotated out of Special Vehicles to the engine lab and then the Advanced Development Lab when Pete's job opened up. The Advanced Development Lab never produced anything useful for production vehicles, but they did develop a computer suspension design program. They worked on a noiseless starter that was always engaged, but that never came to anything. At this point we were working on an external rotor brake. We put the caliper on the inside of the rotor so you could have a bigger diameter rotor. I did some test driving on the freeway for that project. Even though I was released from the rotation part of the CIE program, I still did all the class work and earned a master's degree from the University of Michigan and the Chrysler Institute of Engineering.

I stayed in the Race Group for several years. Hoover was the head of engineering for the drag race group, and Jim Thornton worked for him. Thornton left the department soon after I arrived. One of my earliest assignments was the '68 Hemi A-body car. Hoover was one of the best bosses I ever had because later, after I left the corporation, I was contracted to Chrysler for about ten years doing all of the race engine development work at Keith Black's in Southern California under the guidance of Tom. Hoover would call me and ask, "You think we could do this?" and I'd say, "Yeah, let's try that … " Or I'd say,"Tom, we should be doing this … " and he'd say, "Okay, go ahead and do that …. "

Hoover would come to California every four months, but mostly because he wanted to come to California. He was kind of a hands-on guy because he built his own engines and stuff and so he liked to come there because he said he was jealous that I was able to get all greasy and dirty while he was back in Detroit staying clean.

Meanwhile, back in Detroit. Hoover handed me the job of being in charge of the testing at Milan Dragway. I conned my way into being the test-driver (Jim Thornton had moved on). I developed quite a few things. I was one of the first guys to have a weather station which helped me to come up with a series of correction factors. We couldn't use them for ETs because of the track conditions, but I could correct for trap speed. Hoover would roll into the track at 10 a.m. and walk around, pick the cars to be tested and then maybe leave early. I was driving whatever: Superstocks, B-cars…and factoring in weather conditions, a kid in a candy shop.

THE '68 HEMI A-BODIES

A FEW MONTHS LATER they decided to do the Hemi A-body drag car. Dick Maxwell at that time was working at Product Planning under Bob Cahill. They would guide the Race Group to do what they wanted. Maxwell, Cahill and Hoover came up with the idea of the Super Stock '68 Hemi A-body. We had a meeting and they said, "This is what we want to do … we want to be able to go this fast and do this …"

At that time Hoover had most of the input on what the car should be like, what we'd need for an engine and so forth. He was a great idea guy. Then they told me, "Okay, kid, the car has to weigh X pounds … make the car weigh that much."

I didn't really have much to do with the engines at that time. The engine development was done at the engine lab, and then the engines were sent into the field to be tested. The engine lab development department was not a direct part of the Race Group. There were two or three mechanics who did all the race engine prep in the engine lab, but the engine lab was a separate entity. As I said before, the Race Group had a budget in each department. The engine lab guys had a race budget they worked with to develop the engines. They also had manpower as well as the budget. At that time, Hoover was the Race Group's input with the engine lab engineers. Tom would soon be dubbed the 'Godfather of the Hemi.' They were primarily developing camshafts for the drag race program at that time. The carburettors and manifolds were already pretty much developed as a package, but the cams were being revised constantly.

The other big project was improving head flow. Hoover was pushing the engine lab guys to get more flow out of the heads. As far as cams, Hoover was always on the phone with his buddies at Racer Brown and Crane Cams. Later on, Harvey Crane came up with some analytical approaches to camshaft design, but before that it was: "Okay, try a 265°, 270° ... this, this, this."

You'd try all those, then you'd advance them, then retard them and then you'd mix up the exhaust. It was just piles of camshafts and it was rough work, trial and error. There were very few analytical considerations at that time, they just dyno'd them. They would do the heads, flow the heads, and there weren't any outside sources in California providing their latest and greatest heads because the Hemi was still brand-new. At that time, whatever flow work had to be done was done at Chrysler.

The entire Hemi A-body car program became my job in '67. The first thing I needed to do was make the car weigh X pounds. I always liked the analytical approach, so I gathered as much information as I could about the weights of the cars and individual parts. There was a group in Chrysler that weighed cars. They went out and bought Chevy and Ford products and weighed every nut and bolt. So each department, like the suspension guys, could get a breakdown of what the Ford Mustang's suspension parts weighed—the nuts and bolts, piece by piece. They had a lot of information available for me and the '67 was a new body style.

I collected all this information and made a big chart and started to work on reducing the weight, and especially reducing the weight at the front end of the car. I came up with the fiberglass fenders and hood. There was no acid-dipping at this point, just fiberglass. That was the first head-to-head I had with Maxwell because I went to the meeting and I had it all broken down with what the car was going to weigh and how it was going to look.

Maxwell said, "No, you can't do that, it won't weigh that," and I said, "It will," and so we argued and argued and Hoover said, "Let's try it." I went ahead and did just that and it was spot-on, within a few pounds with distribution and everything.

SUSPENSION DESIGN AND DRAG RACING

I DECIDED THAT I wanted to take an approach to designing the suspension to match the power output. I worked with the suspension lab and that's where I first met Pat Bedard. He had a little drag race car. Bedard didn't drive at that time. His buddy, Lurch, who also worked in the suspension lab, did the wheel time. Bedard struck me as being so out-of-place in the lab. He would come into the lab dressed in a suit and tie and he looked like he came out of GQ—spotless. Everyone else had rolled up sleeves and ties askew. Then one day I found out he was from Iowa and I said, "What's this guy from Iowa doing all slicked up looking like a New Yorker and working in the suspension lab?"

We got to be good friends and we worked out an approach on a rear suspension design. There is a factor of the rear springs called control, the amount of front ratio to back ratio of the springs. It controls the way the rear wheels move longitudinally when they move up and down. I wanted to be able to provide a stable rear suspension without having to do the ladders and all that trick stuff, just with springs. I came up with the rate and the ratios between the left and the right. I did that and, of course, Maxwell says, "That won't work. Our guys won't do that." Not the last time I would hear that.

We built it anyway and went to Irwindale to test. It worked beautifully. Several months later when the first cars were built we went to Cecil County, Maryland, and made the acid test—Ronnie Sox. All the cars I tested were automatics. Maxwell said, "This is never gonna work on a manual transmission."

Ronnie and Buddy were skeptical, Jake King was not. Ronnie and Buddy had a lot of cars and they always had to beef them up. Anyway, our rear suspension worked quite well. Jake was kind of neutral; he was a quiet guy ... however he was the main man. Ronnie was the driver, Buddy was the promoter and Jake was the man behind the car and everything else that moved. It went straight; that was the thing, and it went quite well. It didn't break anything. We had a 9 1/4" rear, a pinion snubber, but nothing external to beef it up. The automatics were 8 3/4" and the manuals were a 9 1/4". Later R&S made some modifications and the car was going faster and faster and proving my basic design. I don't know if they got into the 9s then, but they were in the low 10s, which was pretty awesome for that kind of a car.

Later on we did a lot of the work with the small torque converter. We worked with the lab again and they designed different converters and we tested them and then we'd come back to the lab and say "Do this ... or do that." That's how I got to meet the Spar brothers (B&M) because they were doing most of the converter build-up, even though they were being directed by engineering. Engineering didn't have the facilities to build all those converters, so B&M built them based on what the design group wanted.

CRANKIN' THEM OUT

THE HEMI A-BODY TEST car was completed, and the order came down that they wanted to build 50 Plymouths and 50 Dodges (eventually bumped up to 75 each). At the time, the NASCAR guys were the number-one priority. They got the biggest part of the budget from product planning. When we went to California, I lettered the back of the car: "Nobody Cares." Only a few of us knew what it meant. At Irwindale, Hoover made me cover up the sign up because he didn't want any of the magazine guys taking a photo of the sign and then asking what that meant. It meant that Chrysler didn't care about drag racing because everything went to NASCAR. We got the crap budget. NASCAR had the design group prepare proper drawings. The "drawings" we had of the Hemi A-body were my hand sketches.

When the order came down to build the Hemi A-Bodies, I became a manufacturing engineer. I worked with Brian Schram and Direct Connection, which had a staff of only four or five guys who ordered special parts—mostly for NASCAR but some for drag racing, too. I can't remember all the things we had to order—side glass, lightweight backlight, fiberglass fenders, and hood.

The hood was the biggest problem. I picked a vendor and he couldn't deliver. In fact, with some of the early cars, the guys would come and pick up their cars from Hurst before they had hoods because they weren't made yet. We had to expedite Sox's car because he was number one, and also expedite the second one for Landy.

The A-cars, Barracudas and Darts, were brought over on a wrecker from the Chrysler assembly plant minus engines. Engines came in from M&I (Marine & Industrial) in Maryville, Michigan where they built marine engines and the Hemis. We had a problem that most people probably never heard of, but we lost the first few engines we started up in the Hurst facilities. The manifold bolts were inside the manifold and they broke.

There's a phenomenon called hydrogen embrittlement. You cad-plate the bolts, but after that you have to bake them. If you don't, they'll break because of the internal stresses. Because of the cad-plating, hydrogen soaks in and affects the substructure of the bolt and makes it very brittle. Baking it takes the hydrogen out. It was a well-known phenomenon at that time in engineering circles, but somebody missed it. We had to recall the Hemis and change the manifold bolts. We got the cars out okay, most of the time at the Hurst facilities on 8-Mile Road. At that time, Hurst was really a rat-hole. Later on they built a very nice facility in Ferndale. I got to know the people there.

Dave Landrith was the boss of the Detroit area, and Hurst did a pretty phenomenal thing at that time. They were the first ones to start the specialty car—anything under 2,000 vehicles would be built at Hurst. The first car they did was the 1968 Hurst Olds 4-4-2. The car had to be built outside of GM because GM had promised that they wouldn't build anything with more than 400 cubic inches in an intermediate body, so the 455-cube engine for the Cutlass 4-4-2 had to be installed by Hurst. Truth be told, GM actually installed the 455s at the factory and then shipped the cars to Hurst. Hurst set up a facility next to the plant of the manufacturer they were going to work with. Later on, I worked for Hurst.

The Hemi A-cars went on to be what they are—an incredible success. At one of the early drag meets in California, Hoover, Maxwell and I were wandering through the pits, tending to our flock, when I heard someone shout, "Hey, Turk"! At this point in time my childhood nickname of Turk had not caught up with me. I turned in the direction of the voice, while Hoover and Maxwell kept on walking. The voice belonged to none other than Bill "Farmer" Dismuke, NHRA tech czar, an old friend and fellow member of the Strokers Hot Rod Club from Springfield, Massachusetts. Blast from the past.

I made the introductions and then Farmer said, "I hope I don't find any oxygen bottles in those Hemi cars!!"

We all laughed but the Chrysler blokes didn't get the joke. With much embarrassment, I explained.

When I was a wee lad, circa 1956, I own a 1955 Ford Thunderbird and was constantly getting beat at the local drag strips. One day my imagination runneth over. The IC engine needs air, air is comprised of oxygen, and other things, but oxygen is the mainstay. Sooooo, why not just feed oxygen directly into the engine? Good deal. I fabricated a tube arrangement and attached it to the top of the carburettor and then connected it directly to an oxygen bottle, which I placed in the driver's compartment between the two seats. Add a manual control valve and I was set.

Tuning was a bit crude, which was the embarrassing part, especially for someone who was now 'in the big leagues.' Anyway, I just increased the jet sizes until the engine would barely run on its own, a little lumpy but it would stay lit with a juggling of the throttle. At the starting line, I would rev the engine and turn the manual valve until the engine ran smoothly. Then launch the car, continually modulate the valve with my right hand until it was time to shift, then back to adjusting the valve. I know, I know, not too slick, but remember I was just a novice, so there was still hope, I think. I won a few races, but just a few, before the pistons became a liquefied mess.

Hoover and Maxwell could barely contain themselves. They would not let me forget this blight on my 'record' for some time. But let me remind you of the sage pontification of one Dr. Albert Einstein—"Imagination is more important than knowledge. For knowledge is limited to all we now know and understand, while imagination embraces the entire world, and all there ever will be to know and understand." I rest my case.

When I went to the Chrysler Hemi A-Body reunion in 1993 at Carlisle, Pennsylvania, I was asked many times if I knew it was going to be such a phenomenal car and if I knew it was still going to be around 25 years later. Hell no. I didn't want to belittle the job, but it was a job. I loved the job, driving the test car and all, but I was on the move. I went to the next job and the next. I had no idea what the car would become. If I did, I probably would have kept one for myself. It's worth about $100,000 or so today. I would have kept it in my garage. At the time I probably could have. The whole game was loose, in the industry in general as well as at Chrysler. I could probably have carried away an entire car. I'm sure there were guys who had the same idea. Maybe they didn't take a whole car, but close to that.

THE WAY IT WAS

ONE OF THE INTERESTING things we developed for the Hemi A-body was the Bonzai! Start. That's where you come up to the starting line and bring the engine to about 6,000-8,000 RPM in neutral. I probably started around 6-grand, and then yanked the shifter down into drive. The hardest thing that I had to get used to as a driver was to keep from flinching off the gas. As soon as you pull that lever you want to pull your foot back just a bit, and it took me probably the better part of a day to get my coordination together. At the same time I pulled the shifter, I had to push the throttle down before the lever moved and time that just right so I didn't blow the thing up.

Another time, the lower pulley came off of the engine and I ran over it, blew out the tire and the car spun around slowly at about 130 mph. I caught the rotation and kept off the brakes and just backed it up and backed it all the way down the grass to the finish line at the Detroit Dragstrip. Survival once again. The blame was known but will remain anonymous. We were a loose group of guys, always kidding, fooling around, and it was a really good time in my life.

The Race Group had off-campus facilities located in a defunct Pontiac dealership on Woodward Avenue, a few blocks from Engineering in Highland Park. It was actually on Buena Vista just around the corner from Woodward. We had a station wagon we'd load up with parts and stuff at Engineering. I then generated some loose paperwork and drove the wagon over to our shop on Woodward and worked on the cars. I don't know how much stuff went through there that wasn't supposed to go through there, but we got the job done, no ifs, buts or let me think about thats.

BABY GRAND DART DIVERSION

WHILE I WAS AT Hurst tending to the Hemi A-Body build, I became friends with Dave Landrith, GM of the Detroit operation, and persuaded him to sponsor a race car for yours truly. No local racing for me—I was off to the big time. A 1968 Dodge Dart was put together for the NASAR Baby Grand series, cars, not pianos—which was a precursor to the NASCAR Busch series. I put together a crack team: Dan Mancini, the GM of the Chrysler Woodward Garage; Paul Phelps, master builder of the original Hurst Hemi Under Glass, and Bob 'Turk' Tarozzi, designer, builder, race car engineer, transporter driver, and race car driver.

And we did it right. As I look back through the photographs from that period, I amaze myself. With our small crew, working only nights and weekends, we built a quasi-fixture, drew up real drawings and made real parts and pieces. Now, I will admit that some of the chassis pieces were 'provided' by the suspension lab and a few of the engine parts were 'provided' by the engine lab, and/or Woodward garage remnants. Hey, they gotta go someplace, and we took good care of them. But we, the motley crew, provided the expertise and good old hard labor, far into the night.

We had a crazy painter—aren't they all—at Hurst, and he provided us with the illustrious bumble bee striping. Which, by the way, Chrysler picked up on later for one of their production vehicles. No charge.

The Dart was designed for the oval course, rather than a road course. Engine displacement was limited to 305 cubic inches. The first race was at Bristol Tennessee and I ran up toward the front until the engine blew up—oil pan failure! This was a continuing Achilles heel until NASCAR, years later, allowed teams to switch to a dry sump system. We didn't have a spare engine or funds to rebuild. But my man Dan managed to 'borrow' a complete 340 from the engineering lab. 'Course getting it past tech could prove to be a problem. Brainstorm was in order. NASCAR had just started to use the P&G system to verify the displacement. They would P&G one cylinder and, lo and behold, they let the team pick the cylinder.

Big mistake! If there ever was a motley crew we were it, and devious as well. We drilled a small hole on the underside of the header pipe, then carefully tried several different size welding rods that we slid through the hole and lodged between the exhaust valve head and the valve seat so the valve would not close all the way. With just enough leakage to 'reduce' the displacement we would be home free. Truly a fine example of the old proverb that necessity is the mother of invention.

In the following race at Darlington, I was in second or third place when a caution necessitated a restart. With only about two or three laps left to go I tangled with another competitor. It was bad enough getting stuffed into the wall along the front straightaway, but I had the further misfortune to be photographed in multi-frame glory which then made the front page of the sport section in the *Darlington Daily*. I wasn't planning on all this humiliation, but there it was.

The next couple of races went well, but the finishes were in the middle of the pack somewhere. I can't remember whatever happened to the car, but I was on to bigger and better things? You can be the judge.

4 NASCAR AT CHRYSLER

IN 1968, CHRYSLER'S RACE Product Planning Division was divided, as I remember, into three groups: Scott Harvey, an engineer and the rally guy, was in charge of rallying and road racing (the sporty cars); Bob Cahill headed up drag racing and fuel economy, and Ronnie Householder, who had his own kingdom (and it was a kingdom), was in charge of NASCAR activities.

Pete Hutchinson had returned from Car and Driver and was working with Scott Harvey on a few different projects, although he was officially working under Ronnie Householder. Earlier there was an oddball 4-wheel independent suspension Chrysler race car that they had built. It didn't go anywhere and it didn't do anything, but they did drive it around.

Hutchinson wanted to go sporty car racing and he proposed a Trans-Am car; this would've been in early '68 or late '67. They went over to engineering with Tom Hoover and those guys and talked about how they were going to do it. Larry Rathgeb was in charge of the engineering end of NASCAR, but he was overloaded with work and I think most of the guys knew I had the feeling for sports cars and sporty cars. I had done my master's thesis on suspension analysis and vehicle control, and I could get things done. I had spent a season with Scott Harvey and the Team Starfish effort, 1966 Plymouth Barracuda Trans Am racing. And hey, I had all that NASCAR experience in the Baby Grand!

So they gave me the job—I was in charge of the project. It didn't have a budget yet, so they just said, "We want a car." Hutch's approach was, "Let's get started." He had some ideas about which car it was going to be—it was supposed to be the new-for-'70 E-body Barracuda that was going to be our mule test car. I started the engineering and design studies for the 'Cuda which was in the works at the time. There was no metal but we had designs; we weren't actually building any cars yet. I worked for a few months doing this job and I think we had less funding than what we wanted or we couldn't get the full budget so we just stopped the project. Done.

BIRTH OF THE NASCAR CHARGER

SO NOW I'M SORTA out of a job, but Larry Rathgeb says, "Kid, how would you like to build a NASCAR car?"

I said, "Beautiful, how do we do that?"

He said, "Here's some drawings." He hands me this big roll of drawings. "Here's the keys to an Imperial, and here's the address of Ray Nichels' place in Indiana. Go down and build this race car."

This was a very special '68 Dodge Charger (a race prototype). This all happened in the matter of an hour. This prototype Dodge Charger was the version before the Daytona wing car. It was a Charger 500 with the filled-in backlight and flush headlights and grille.

I went home to my wife and told her I was going down to Indiana. "I don't know where Indiana is but I'm going there." I was maybe 31. Larry never introduced me to the Nichels operation. He just sent me down there.

THE NICHELS CONNECTION

I SHOW UP WITH all these drawings and even in those days, Ray Nichels' place was a first-class operation, along with Paul Goldsmith and all. The mechanics and the shop were really outstanding. They had built hundreds of cars, maybe more. At Nichels' shop they must've been looking at me, this kid, and wondering what's going on. Then I laid out all these drawings. The major part of this project was that the Chrysler body design group had designed the rollcage. It was a special rollcage based on extensive stress analysis, the first time they had done that, and I was supposed to build that into a car. I wasn't fabricating, I was just the boss.

This was actually the second Dodge Charger 500 test mule. The first vehicle preceded my delicate handiwork and was affectionately referred to as #046. The primary difference between #046 and the current vehicle in the works, DC-93, was the body-to-floor pan tilt of 1.5 degrees. This rake angle change had been carefully worked out by the aero guys back at the works. Top secret. There were other mods that are outlined below but this was the most significant one.

Around the middle of the DC-93 build, sometime in September 1968, I was summoned to participate in a test at Daytona of the #046 test mule. This was actually a prelim to learn about the general behavior of the race car at Daytona using a limited amount of instrumentation. There were a small number of channels of data available, so we spent most of the time viewing the yaw angle channel. The most significant difference between #046 and DC-93 was that #046 had no floor-pan rake. The highest test speeds obtained during this test was approximately 186 mph. Test conditions where not ideal but the car was very stable, which in itself was a major accomplishment.

Meanwhile back at Nichels they had given me a first-class crew. Nichels was contracted with Chrysler to do prototype work. They rolled out the red carpet. We started to work and they gave me all their best guys. I was okay in their eyes, because I had worked in the field and I worked well with people who work well. I respected them and they respected me.

I didn't even realize until I got down there what we were going to do. They had Charger bodies-in-white. They were uni-body cars—no frame. The first thing they did was un-weld the whole body (I didn't even know we were doing that until I read the prints and the drawings), and then we had to tilt the body sheet metal on the uni-body floor pan 1-1/2 degrees for aerodynamics. They un-spot-welded everything, tipped it nose down and then welded it back on. I'm thinking, "These guys are good!"

Then they start putting in the rollcage and one of the guys says, "This over here, what are they doing that for?"

And I'd say, "Well, we gotta do it for this reason and that reason."

And they'd say, "How about we do this?"

And I'd say. That looks good. Do it!"

They liked it because I would never call back to HQ—I hardly ever called, they didn't call me and I didn't call them. We became good working mates and then we came to the big event.

THOSE P.I.T.A. BARS

IN THE ENGINE COMPARTMENT, the body design group had put in two diagonal bars which came essentially from the center of the hood opening, or fender upper rail, where the shock support bars were, to the center of the engine bulkhead. They were referred to as the 'Pain In The Ass' bars because, as drawn, they would not allow the engine or valve covers to be removed—or installed, for that matter. The body design group had just put them in there, welded them in place, so to speak.

The first guy says, "How are we going to get the engine in and out of there?"

I said, "You are right, but we have to have those bars, they're important structural members."

One guy said, "How about we take this bar, flatten out the ends, and then put these nuts and bolts in there?"

I said, "Beautiful. Let's do it."

They're removable. It was things like that that went well. Nobody ever came down from Detroit to see the car the whole time I was building it. Of course, I went to the Daytona tests and I think I went back to Detroit a few times, but that was before digital cameras so I didn't take any pictures. Just progress reports and schedules. (Are you on time? Are you on time? Are you on time?)

The other thing I did was to work it out with the engine lab to put a motor plate on the engine. The motor plate went between the block and the water pump. It's not like it was a first—Can-Am cars have used them, Formula cars have used them, but I just thought it was a great way to put the engine in and out, and add a little stiffness to the overall structure. I worked out the design with the lab guys who were building the engine back in Detroit for us here in Indiana. The engine came with the engine plate installed. Today everybody knows them as 'Elephant Ears.'

GRINDING OUT THE NUMBERS

GEORGE WALLACE WORKED FOR Chrysler Corp. He didn't officially work for the Race Group, but he was like an analytical brainiac and there was his pepper grinder. It was before desktop computers, and the pepper grinder was this two inch diameter, four inch tall calculator with a crank handle on the top, and you'd do magical things with it. I never even knew how to work it. You'd set certain things, grind it and numbers would just pop-up on its cylindrical surface. While this device was commonly known as a pepper grinder calculator, its proper name was the Curta Calculator*. There's even a YouTube video showing how to use it.

* Designed in the mid-1930s by Curt Herzstark of Vienna, and perfected at the Buchenwald concentration camp (also by Herzstark) under the Nazis—RLT.

George worked at the road test garage and his job was to predict vehicle performance based on car weights, weight distributions, powertrain specs and power curves. That's what he did for production cars, and then they'd go to the proving grounds and test the vehicle, and then he'd come back and adjust the program for tire inflations, weather conditions etc., and he worked on that over the years. He was also a race enthusiast—nut is more like it—and he would do numerous side projects.

When the Mobil Economy Run was on, George was there. There's an optimum way to drive the car for economy. George came up with this little ramp in the ashtray with a marble in it, so if the driver maintained the marble's position in a certain place that would indicate optimum acceleration. And they got away with it for a couple of years because the drivers were not supposed to have any aids to drive the car, so it was probably illegal. The really interesting part was that there was a USAC official in the back seat, and he apparently never noticed.

I didn't participate in those projects; I just heard these stories afterwards. George and I would often scratch our heads together. There was a phenomenon that was published in some of the Grand Prix books. The lap time of a race car was a function of the sixth root of its power. He wanted to verify that. We had the engine lab run the same Hemi engine with four different carburettors so we got four different power levels. This would then allow us to compare lap times at different power levels, and hopefully verify the sixth root rule.

"I QUIT!"

Larry Rathgeb and I had the same belief that we could set up the car on paper. We did just that. We got some scales to determine the wheel weights and picked and selected the springs and the roll bar combinations, and we had a way of balancing the roll couple front-to-rear and predicting the handling qualities and capabilities of the car. So the car was all set up on paper. So back at Nichels' place we got this all done. The car's all painted and it's like the night before we're ready to go to Daytona from Indiana for testing. This was now late in November. Householder (God himself), Pete Hutchinson—who was a friend of mine—and Larry Rathgeb all show up in Indiana and say … I forget exactly how it went … Householder essentially said, "This car is no good, my racers have looked at it, Petty in particular and some other guys (mind you, nobody had looked at the car itself), and it won't work. The pain-in-the-ass bars (I think that's where the name came from for the first time), they can't work with those, and the motor plate's gonna leak. They don't want to race with the motor plate."

I said, "Wait a minute, first of all you haven't even looked at the car, the pain-in-the-ass bars are removable …"

Then he said, "Well, we don't want them in there, they're not gonna do any good."

I said, "This is an engineering test car, we're supposed to be testing new ideas. If it doesn't work, then you don't incorporate it. If it does work and you don't want to incorporate it, so be it. But you can't tell me that I shouldn't go test this stuff because that's my job. What else would I be doing here?"

So I'm ranting and raving like a 30-year old kid would do, and Rathgeb—my boss—isn't backing me up. I was really surprised at this. Most of this stuff was probably his idea in the first place. My buddy Pete

Hutchinson is siding with Householder because he works for Householder. So finally I say, "Screw it," (a little coarser than that actually), and I walked out. "I quit!"

I go back to the hotel. Now the plot thickens. Previously I had worked with Hurst on building the so-called 'production' Hemi A-body drag car and my little Dodge racer. From time to time they wanted me to do different projects for them as a consultant on the side. I had said, "I don't know, I'm pretty busy."

But at this point I called up Dave Landrith at Hurst and told him I could use the job. He said it was great because they were in the process of building the AMX drag race car, the competitor to (well, it was a different class, I think) the Hemi A-Body Barracuda. I said, "Okay, well, here's what you do. Go to this spring manufacturer, buy these springs, do this, do that …." I told him I'd talk to him and we'd get together when I got back to Detroit.

I UNQUIT (TEMPORARILY)

I HANG UP THE phone, there's a knock on the door and Rathgeb walks in. He said, "What are you doing, you can't quit."

I said I sure could and we went on and on. Finally he's presenting the argument that I have to go to Daytona and test the car because only I know all the details, including a few tricks that I had put into the car specifically for this test. Apparently, they'd agreed that we could test it. Rathgeb must've come alive at that time and pushed for testing the car although Householder said he won't use it even if it worked, but Larry tells me I gotta go down and test the car. It was politically very muddy.

Rathgeb kept telling me I gotta go to Daytona because I have this engine comparison to do and all the chassis work. I guess he didn't feel comfortable going down and doing the testing not having built the car. I never understood that. I said, OK because in the back of my mind I remembered that the Hurst guys with the AMX car project told me they were going to be at Crane's (Crane Cams) place in Florida (close to Daytona) to do the engine work at the same time as building the car.

So I told Larry I'd go and do the test, then I'd quit when we got back to Detroit.

As soon as he leaves I call up Landrith and I say, "Dave, when are you going to Florida? Because here's the deal: I'll be in Florida in Daytona doing this car test thing and Crane's in Hollywood, Florida; it's just down the street. I can meet you there and do the AMX job."

He says that's good. I go down to Daytona, do the test and it went just like perfect—mid-190s right out of the trailer. We put the pain-in-the-ass bars in and out. Buddy Baker was the test driver. I remember that he was the only driver that I ever worked with who would test blind; that is, let us make changes without telling him what the changes were. We took the bars out, put them in, and took them out again. He noticed the difference. We noted the variations in the data we collected as well. This was only the second attempt at collecting onboard data and it was starting to really come together.

> <u>Time-Shift</u>—*Larry Rathgeb*
> *Circa 2011*—In an email correspondence I had with Larry, unrelated to what follows, I received this unsolicited declaration, " ... ... That aside, I am still trying to forget that stinging Householder comment; 'We didn't hire you bastards, you just grew on us.' But as you said, that's another story. You always did have a short fuse like the rest of us whose names end with a vowel (my mother's maiden name was Rinaldo). Many times I regret not having left Nichels' office in front of you."—Thank you Larry, you're the man!

CHRYSLER PIONEERS DATA ACQUISITION

DATA ACQUISITION IN 1968 was interesting. Chrysler had a group of people who did the Apollo moon shot—Saturn booster, or something like that. They were out of a job at that point in time and there was a group of three or four guys from one of the departments down there who were also NASCAR nuts, and they made a proposal to the race group that they could develop a data acquisition package. At that point, nobody had anything like this; there was nothing out there.

They did one thing that was really phenomenal and to this day I have not found anything to replace it. They made a yaw meter. It was a pot-type sensor (potentiometer), about as big as a coffee cup, a frictionless pot essentially, with about a 3/8-inch diameter shaft sticking up out of it, and about five inches long. The shaft had a slot in it. We bolted the base to the roof of the race car and then the shaft stuck up through the roof. The body of the pot sensor would turn, or rotate, with the car, but the shaft would turn with the wind, so now you have your yaw angle (the difference between the angle of the car itself and the angle it is traveling). In addition to that gizmo, the space guys gave us a brush recorder. It's like the machine used in a lie detector test, with the little needles going back and forth on moving paper. This box was probably about ten or twelve inches long and six inches wide and five or six inches tall. It was a pretty big piece.

We put it in the trunk or back seat of the car and we oriented the brushes (needles) so they were lateral and be least affected by centrifugal force. We bolted it into the car and then fed paper through the surface plate and then we had a little catch bracket or cage that would collect the paper. We just started the car up and drove it around the track and the brush recorders would record. We had three or four channels so we could record yaw, engine speed, throttle position, brake pressure, whatever we wanted. That yaw meter was able to detect the change in yaw angle when we took the pain-in-the-ass bars in and out and it correlated exactly to what Baker told us it was doing on the track. Bottom line: the car had less rotation with the bars in place. Yes ma'am!

At that time, the downforce was primarily created by a combination of the 1-1/2 degree angle between the body and the floorpan and the height of the rear deck spoiler, along with the length of the front spoiler. Baker was able to go around Daytona flat-out during testing and never had to lift off the throttle. It was a good test because if he had to lift, then something was wrong with the car. We worked with the height of the deck spoiler and put the pain-in-the-ass bars in and out of the car, different things like that. We also were able to do the carburettor testing because, again, going flat-out, the speed of the car was a function of the engine power—that's it. The driver was essentially out of the equation. The car was that stable thanks to those pain-in-the-ass bars. George Wallace was able to verify the sixth root equation. He was so happy, he was, like, in heaven.

The motor plate never leaked, but alas, I don't believe it was ever used in a NASCAR race car, maybe. The pain-in-the-ass bars are still used to this day, as is the rear deck spoiler. Data acquisition packages are used by everyone, everywhere, except now they are micro-sized compared to what we started with. Ah, how times have changed. Right after that I left and went to Hollywood—Florida that is, and did the AMX drag race engine project for Hurst.

The '68 Charger 500 evolved into the '69 Charger Daytona, complete with the worlds tallest wing, which went on to totally dominate NASCAR.

5 DRAG RACING AND NASCAR AT HURST

After I completed the Chrysler NASCAR Charger 500 project, I went to work for Hurst to build an engine for the AMC AMX drag race car. Before that, other than my own engine work that I had done when I was a kid building my own engines (and I never really had a dynamometer so I wasn't able to do any dyno work), I did a lot of drag racing, roundy-round racing and that kind of stuff on my own. I spent a little bit of time in the engine lab when I was at Chrysler, but I hadn't done a lot of hands-on engine design or development work.

Now I had to develop this engine for Hurst. Typical operation—the Hurst crew shows up at Harvey Crane's place in Florida with the rear springs in the truck and car half-built. They were finishing the car in the back of the shop while I was doing the engine development in the dyno room. Beforehand, they had asked me to predict the car's performance and I had predicted that it would go 11.25 at 125 mph.

The first thing I did was to get on with the engine program. AMC had their chief engineer there who had designed the engine we were using, so I was under a little pressure. The engine was a three-something, not a 305, like a 360 or 390, whatever their standard size was at the time. The first thing that happened was we kept losing oil pressure. We'd run it up a little bit and the oil pressure would go away.

I don't know why I started looking at the oil pump. (Intuition pointed me in that direction I guess.) One of the first things I noticed was that the oil pump body was aluminum and essentially a part of the front cover, which was also aluminum. And they were using steel gears. So I figured the body must be expanding, resulting in yards of clearance.

We ended up sanding down the pump body and making a net cold fit (zero clearance) between the body and the gears. A little dicey, but workable. I put the gears in the pump body/cover and sanded everything down because we didn't really want to take the engine apart. We just buffed it up so that the gears actually touched the cover when you put it together.

What was happening was that AMC had some spec of 10 or 20 thousandths clearance. Put the aluminum cover on and heat it up and you've now got 100 thousandths, or whatever. We made the fix and man, the chief engineer thought I was the smartest guy in the world. This was an engine that had been around for a while; it wasn't brand new. "Oh, man, my guys never figured that out."

We went on and the engine ran pretty good. We tried a number of Harvey Crane's camshafts, and the engine must've had dual quads on it I would suspect, but I don't remember the output. We finished the car, put the engine in and went to the local dragstrip and ran 11.25, 125 mph! (Who needs computers?) It was the first time I drove a stick car. Before that it was all automatics. It went right up there to where it was supposed to be. Hurst went ahead and built the cars for AMC. Shirley Shahan (a.k.a. the Drag-On Lady) had one of the first cars. Her and her husband, H.L., had campaigned one of the Hemi A-Body cars for Chrysler in 1968 and she went over to AMC in 1969.

The AMC AMX project got me in deep, deep crap with Chrysler. I'd quit the corporation, but Bob Cahill was very upset with me because he figured I'd stolen all the stuff that they'd developed. I felt bad because I liked Cahill and I didn't want those guys at Chrysler to be mad at me.

So when I got back to Detroit (I'm not generally a politician), I called "Mr. Cahill" and I said, "Let's go to lunch." Me, taking this guy (the boss) to lunch. I tried to explain to him that what I did on the Hemi A-Body, first of all, was my idea to do the rear suspension the way I did it. And because the car was jacked up quite high in the front, the front suspension required some fancy NASCAR-type treatment. In fact, when I went to California to drive it, the car was all over the place; I could hardly go straight. This was a phenomenon called bump-steer. Drag racers didn't know about that stuff, but because I had a suspension background, I knew what it was.

When I came back I wanted to make new steering arms. Dick Maxwell said no way, it's too expensive, we'll just have the guys bend them. I said no, bad deal. Let's just make a new steering arm. He finally agreed and the cars went nice and straight. I had done that on the AMX because I was privy to that information. I knew bump-steer would happen once you brought the car up in the air. The AMX was fairly successful and I tried to explain to Cahill what my thoughts were and my feelings about what I did. Of course I told him the story about Householder. Householder and he were not buddies because there was just one pot of money. The sporty car guys would try to get their money, the drag race guys would try to get their money, and Householder was the king, the Chrysler Stock Car/NASCAR czar, and he got the big portion of the pot, so he was not a friend of Cahill's and Cahill would always get his leftover crumbs, so to speak. We left on speaking terms and then time healed all wounds.

After I did the AMX car for Hurst I went to work for them. Hurst gave me a fancy office. Another attraction to working for Hurst was that they said if I came on board with them, they would be able to get the AMC Trans-Am program for '69. Now you're talking! I get my suit back on and we go down to AMC and sit down for our meeting, and "Oh, by the way, we already gave our Trans-Am program to a couple of guys from Pennsylvania, Mark Donohue and Roger Penske."

I'm pissed off now because I came to Hurst specifically to do that job, but, "as a consolation prize, we want to put the Javelins in the NASCAR Baby Grand series."

I said that sounds cool, we'll build two cars. I'll drive one, we'll get another name driver, and off we'll go. But now I got to see the car. I didn't even know what the car looked like. I see the car, a Javelin. The engine was a derivative of the engine we had done for the AMX car, but it was a special built 305—so it was a downsized 360, whatever it was. And it's got a trunnion/kingpin front end, a throwback to the horseless carriage era.

We asked for what little help we could get in terms of drawings and things like that because I had to completely redesign the front suspension, but I said, "Okay, we'll do it." Here again, it's just phenomenal how things came together in those days. Listen closely.

I had been away from Chrysler for maybe almost a month or so. In redesigning the AMC front suspension, I had to redo the whole thing. I took out the stock stuff and reinforced the frame. I had to build upper and lower control arms and a spindle, straight forward. Then I thought, "What am I gonna do for a spindle?" There were a lot of special spindles that we had made at Chrysler that were gonna go in the Trans-Am engineering car, but then never made it into the car, because we'd never built the Trans-Am engineering car. They're just lying around at engineering. So how about if I lean on some of my buddies to get some spindles?

Somehow I was able to get those spindles out of Chrysler Engineering and incorporate them in the Javelin car. It sounds like a fairy tale, but that's what happened. I redesigned the whole suspension, put in adjustable coil springs, built the upper and lower control arms, steering and all that crapola. Paul Phelps, Hemi Under Glass, my Dodge Baby Grand project, among other Hurst creations, was my main man. We had to design and fabricate everything. There was very little of the original Javelin left.

I rounded up about six neophytes to the racing business and construction was underway. I got pretty dirty on this one myself. Time was of the essence. The engine required a major visionary approach, but somehow we got it all done. Racers always make it under the wire.

Before Jaguar, in '66 Bob Tullius was Dodge-sponsored, sort of. In '66 Bob had two guys on his team. Chrysler was helping him a little bit. Enter Team Starfish. We had two of the fastback Barracudas and we were campaigning them on the same circuits. T/S were Chrysler guys, a group of engineers that I had hooked up with, a group that Scott Harvey had organized. We had like six, eight, ten guys who would go to the races. So we helped Bob as well because he only had two guys doing all the pit stops and stuff.

I didn't realize until I talked to Tony Adamowitz not long ago here at the historic car races (Tony used to drive for Bob), that Bob raced in '67 and it turns out that this Dodge, which was driven by Tullius, was the only Chrysler Trans-Am car to ever win races. His #4 was a Trans-Am Dodge Dart. Many people probably don't know about that car. He campaigned it in '66, and then campaigned it in '67. By '67 I was doing other things so I lost track of it. Adamowitz reminded me that Bob won at least two races, maybe three. Bob's guys built that car. It wasn't much to build race cars in those days, a knuckle, a few springs, some engine pieces; which he got from Chrysler. He was sponsored by Chrysler, but to a very little extent—no decals, more of an independent. As I said they gave him engine parts, they gave him a few brakes, oh, and they gave him an oil pan that didn't work.

So when the AMC Javelin came to be, I asked Bob if he'd like to drive for me. I was going to drive one car and he could drive the other. As race time approached we only had the one car finished. The first race of the season for this car was called the Paul Revere 250. It started in the afternoon and ran for 250 miles, and it was on the road course at Daytona. So I gave the ride to Bob.

All the other drivers were mainly roundy-round guys. I don't remember where we qualified, probably on or near the pole. First lap in the road course at Daytona, Bob's going into turn one and the rest of the guys are coming out of turn four—that's how much of a lead he had on the first lap. Phenomenal. We're going and everything's great and all of a sudden, the Javelin comes in and it's making a funny burbling noise; and here's a story that's again like a fairy tale. Facts are indeed stranger than fiction.

Right away Paul Phelps and I open the hood and we could smell the fuel—something wrong with the carburettor. Brilliant. The fuel was all flooding out of the front bowl, so I unscrewed the bowl. The float had cracked, the tang had broken off. Now, how many times do you take float bowls to the racetrack—never.

I turn around and there's a guy who I knew quite well who was the Holley representative for Chrysler NASCAR. He was always at the NASCAR races, tuning up Holley carburettors for all the Chrysler race cars. I'm standing there with this broken bowl in my hand wondering what am I going to do, and out of the blue my guy comes in with a complete bowl assembly, assembled with the screws, the gaskets, the o-rings, the whole nine yards. And he hands it to me. He knew, he just heard the sound, and he was there. He brings this kit over and I just go, "Oh." I slap it on, screw it in, off we go, turn around and I never saw him again (a much belated thank you to Gary Congdon (a.k.a. Ed U). The car finished, but I can't remember where it finished. It was just okay.

That was the first race. Then we went to the next race and Bob, he never did roundy-round stuff before, got punted out of the racetrack and over the fence. I thought, holy cow, he's dead. But he was okay. One thing after another, we never had the chance to build the second car for yours truly and my driving career from there just went downhill, which was one of the saddest parts of my life.

Enough. My next adventure was building a Trans Am car for Chrysler.

6 LIFE AT ALL AMERICAN RACERS

HERE'S THE WAY THE Trans Am program came about. I had done some preliminary Trans Am design work at Chrysler in 1967. The current program actually started off with Pete Hutchinson saying once again, "Let's build a sporty car." He was looking to utilize some of the components he had developed for the Indy program on the small-block, which was basically a 340 at that time. It was 1969 and I was working for Hurst doing the NASCAR Baby Grand Javelin program. For the last race of the year (it was an invitational race), we were invited to the Mexico City Formula One race to do a prelim event. This was a mixed bag where we ran against some of the Mexican modified Grand Touring cars. They were plastic bodies and tube frames with big (400-cube) engines.

I knew I wasn't going to stay at Hurst because this was only a one-year program and they weren't going to renew it. They wanted me to do some of the concept cars. I had done a few with them, but that wasn't my thing. I just wanted to go racing. So I thought that on my way back I would send everyone else home from Mexico City to Detroit. But I took a flight from Mexico City to Southern California, where I spent a few days going around and talking to some people that I knew to see if I could find a job in California. Sort of like a chess game, thinking several moves ahead.

CALIFORNIA DREAMING

I WENT TO SEE several people and then somehow I ended up going over to see Pete Hutchinson at Keith Black's place, where he was doing the engine development for the Trans Am project, which I hadn't been aware of. He was originally stationed there to do the Indy race engine program and now he was just starting into the Trans Am. There was no car at this point;

they had an engine before they had a car. They knew they were going to do the car, Product Planning had approved it, both Plymouth and Dodge divisions, and it was in the works. I showed up not knowing any of this was happening.

Pete said, "I've been thinking about you. How'd you like to work for Dan Gurney?" or, "How'd you like to do a Trans-Am race car?" I forget exactly how he put it. "Gurney's looking for a chassis guy, somebody to design their chassis."

I immediately drove to AAR and talked to Dan. I also talked to Max Muhleman, who was kind of his general manager and PR guy.

Hutch had obviously briefed them and they said, "Okay, we'll let you know."

So I made a few other stops and then went back home to Detroit. This was right before Christmastime. It was December in Detroit and my wife and I were then living in a rented house, and by this time we had two little munchkins, Bobby, and Kristine.

A couple of days later I got a phone call and Gurney said, "We want to hire you. When can you get out here?"

Well, this to me was now a golden opportunity for a couple of reasons: one, I was going to work in the big time, and two, I was going to California. No more winters in Detroit. That was my goal from way back, just get to California.

I said to my wife Liz, "They want me there the next week. That means you gotta pack up and …"

Fortunately we didn't own the house but she had to sublet. She said, "Okay. I'll do that." That's my gal!

They also agreed to fly her out once or twice to look for a house, and part of the deal was they were going to give me a car and all that cool stuff … stars in my eyes.

THE CHRYSLER CONNECTION

At our meeting in California Hutch had said, "By the way, before you come out here, go over to engineering and pick up all the drawings and stuff that you did a couple of years ago."

Although I was not a current Chrysler employee, I still had my Engineering ID card, so I walked up to the gate at Highland Park, flashed my card and walked right into Engineering. Just look like you know what you're doing. Then I went to see the guys in the suspension design group and asked, "You guys still got those rear suspension layouts, control arm drawings, those knuckles and all that stuff?" We had developed components for the Trans Am car in that short period in '67 right before they canned the project. I was finding out if they were still in the bin.

I collected the drawings and some of the analyses that we did. I think we even had a computer run or two—which was cutting-edge. Chrysler did have a computer in those days, a monster IBM 360. I think it was a data-processing computer located in a separate building. The way we did suspension analysis was to fill out a sheet which looked like the IBM punch cards, not the actual cards, put in numbers and send them in an inter-department mailer over to the financial building and they would run them at night. That was the only time they had time to run engineering work on the computer. The results would be on your desk in the morning. You would check the results and if any changes were needed you would redo the data sheet and back it would go into the mail system. Later we used a program that the advanced development group was just starting to work on. This program was done in BASIC; the IBM 360 program was written in Fortran.

During one of my CIE rotations I was working in the advanced development group. I was assigned a task to devise a subroutine, me with no computer training in college, for ball joint angularity. I got it done, and then they added that as a subroutine to the main program. They were just starting to do that kind of work, and you would get a plot and the plot would be all X's and O's. It was a very basic plot, no fancy graphics like we have today. So I had some of those analyses, some drawings, spring rates and anti-roll bar specifications. I collected that stuff, but I did have to go see somebody to get signed out. I slid in okay but I knew I'd be in handcuffs if I tried to sneak out with an armful of drawings.

I got on the plane from Detroit and I got out to California at around 9:30 or 10:00 p.m. This is like 12:30 to 1:00 am Detroit time. Somebody from All American Racers picks me up at the airport and brings me to All American Racers, and they want to start working right away. It's almost Christmas time and I find out they want to have a test in March because there was a race at Laguna Seca in April. So there was no time to waste.

Then they give me a bunch of jack: "Oh, we're gonna build a building for you, where do you want your office, yada yada?"

And they showed me the building plans. So all this stuff is going on and it's 1:00 am. on my first day there. Welcome to the big time, 24/7. Little did I know that eventually I would not only design the car, but assist in the buildup of both the Plymouths and Dodges, become the Plymouth team manager and the race engineer. Talk about wearing an assortment of hats. Holy s**t. BTW, this was 1970. I don't even know if the term race engineer existed yet.

ALL AMERICAN RACERS

I WENT RIGHT TO work and I had to take the remnants of the drawings that I got from Chrysler—they weren't complete drawings, mainly layouts—and then transfer them into drawings at All American Racers so we could start making parts. All the engine parts were being gathered and all that stuff was being done at Keith Black's place.

Nothing was being done at All American Racers until I showed up. They did not have a fixture big enough to put a car on. The cars hadn't even arrived yet, but we had to build a fixture big enough to put them on. Don't forget all the previous work down at AAR was on wee cars, like Indy, Formula A and Can-Am cars. Our cars would be bodies-in-white pulled out of the assembly plant. This was December 1969, the E-bodies were in production at that time and the races would be in '70. First thing is, we gotta build a fixture. Most importantly, they gave me Phil Remington. Remington is a craftsman personified. He was with everybody. He's still down at Gurney's futzing around, but he's in his mid-90s now. They gave him to me, so to speak. "Here is your helper." He's like in his 50s and I'm in my 30s and he's my helper … yeah, right. He took it OK.

<u>Time-Shift</u>—*Phil Remington*

I have to jump ahead for just a moment to reveal the real Phil Remington. Just a short while ago, 2013, I was given a book to read regarding the Ford LeMans effort in the 1960s, Go Like Hell by A. J. Blains. Buried deep in the text were precious gems that showed who Phil Remington really was, and let's just call him Rem! The text alluded to numerous assets that Rem brought to the program, but one struck a chord with my gray cells.

For the 1966 LeMans effort, Ford had shoehorned the Ford 427 V8 into the GT 40. It was front-heavy for sure, but it could go like hell! Everyone felt that braking longevity for the 24 hours of LeMans would lead to disaster. Not Rem. He devised a rotor quick-change system allowing the team to change rotors and calipers in minutes. The flat rate time would've been hours. The officials thought perhaps, maybe, it was illegal, but they never acted upon it. The rest, as they say, is history.

Had I known what an icon Rem really was, I'm sure I would have approached our relationship differently. Although, by treating him as one of the guys I think our relationship developed as one of mutual respect. More on this down the page a bit. (See **- I'm In, I'm Out Again!—The Layoff***)*

WE'RE BUILDING TAXICABS

REMINGTON WAS A REALLY cool guy. He got more stuff done than I did, and I got a lot of stuff done. He said, "We gotta build a fixture."

I said, "Okay, we can build it out of tubular … ."

He said,"No, no! We'll get these I-beams, we'll weld them together, we'll send them out and have them Blanchard ground."

"Oh, okay, let's do that"

So he goes off and does that. Our cars were referred to as "taxicabs." Compared to what they were building at AAR, the term was appropriate. Some of the guys on the AAR workforce didn't really want to come and work for us on the Trans-Am cars because they were not sophisticated. All American Racing was doing Indy cars, the Dan Gurney Eagles. Our cars were indeed taxicabs compared to that stuff. They had a complete facility there for fabricating "real" race cars—Formula One cars, Can-Am, but mostly they were building Indianapolis cars—aluminum—all very high-quality craftsmanship.

Remington was one of the super craftsmen in the place, and he was an all-around guy. He wouldn't work in any one department. He was worse than me as far as wearing hats. He had worked for Shelby. He had done Shelby Mustangs and came up through that. He had a bag full of hammers and dollies, and every once in a while he'd take one out and say something like, "This formed the nose section on the 1950 Indy car …" for somebody or other. He had more stories than you could imagine. But in the end he was an expediter of the first order. He wasn't a graduate engineer, as far as I knew, but he knew as much, if not more, about engineering than I did. But, he was extremely short on patience.

One of the things Remington did as we got into the program was to decide we needed to have a race car brake and clutch combo, and the brakes had to have a balance bar to adjust the front and rear portioning. They didn't have those available off the shelf so he made one up. He started a layout of the assembly, so he had the brake pedal and the cylinders and all that. The more conventional way of making drawings was once you make the assembly layout, you put that sheet aside and you make a drawing of the clutch pedal and the brake pedal, and you get another drawing and you make the brackets, like that. Well, he would do everything on one piece of paper. He would go over there and then do a projection over here and do the brake pedal and the clutch pedal, and then go back over there and do the sheetmetal.

What happened was that some of the pieces would have to be made in the machine shop and some of the pieces would have to be made in the sheetmetal shop. Remington was quite an ornery character, but he had a lot of respect throughout the shop. They wouldn't say, "Hey, Phil, you gotta make drawings to go in the machine shop and another set of drawings to go in the sheetmetal shop." They'd just run off his assembly layout and then they carefully cut out the selections and send the sheetmetal pieces to the sheetmetal shop and the machine pieces to the machine shop. That's how much they feared (respected) him there. Later on, he was assigned to train some of our guys, which was an education to say the least.

We couldn't get but a couple of guys to come over from the Indy program to work for us. We ended up hiring some of the crew from Shelby's Trans Am program from the previous season, and some young kids who didn't know anything yet. Remington's job was to train these kids. They each worked on a car and they did all the work in the shop, but eventually they were going to go with me on the road as crew guys. We were hoping to pick the best to do the better jobs. He would show guys welding, for instance, but he had zero tolerance. He would show you how to do something, and if you did it, and you did it right, you were in his good graces and you were his buddy. If you didn't do it right, he'd push you aside, do it himself, and then never speak to you again. He was tough.

Fortunately, I must've done a few things right because he and I became reasonably good friends. When I went on the road we designed parts by sketches on napkins and phone conversations. The parts fit on the car and they were beautiful. Two examples were the wheel lug nut retainers and the Plum (balls) cooler that brought outside air to the driver. All the other competitors had them for the next race after we installed them. We communicated well at some level. He stayed at the shop; he was the shop guy and so he ultimately did all that shop work.

Remington sent out the fixture and had it made, and meanwhile we're doing drawings of the chassis. Dan had two draftsmen, one was Roman

Slabovinski, who was just starting at AAR and later became an Indy Car designer and did some award-winning cars. But at that time he was straight out of the aircraft industry and knew nothing about race cars. He was assigned to do that year's Indy car for Dan. Lynn Terry was the designer and he would come in and point some fingers and fly back to England. That's a story in itself for another time.

They gave me the AAR engine guy to do my chassis drawings, Richard Lynhurst. Fortunately, he and I got along well and it wasn't that difficult, so we went ahead and started making drawings. The early drawings we did from sketches I had made. I was preparing to do control arms, so we were starting there. The cars show up and they go onto the fixture. The first car was sent out to be acid-dipped and then put on the fixture. The first car was to be a Plymouth; second car was to be a Dodge; the third car was Plymouth and the fourth car a Dodge. The first car was the test car; it had to be ready for March to go testing at Riverside. We got started and got our crew in and our workers; and we proceeded to build the car.

SO WHERE'S THE ENGINE?

WE'RE INTO JANUARY AND maybe starting to get to February, building the cars, going along fairly well except for the usual problems—can't get these parts and springs and so forth. But overall we're humming along. Dan had an engine guy named John Miller who was the most non-communicative guy that I have ever known in my life. He would sit at meetings and grunt and not say anything. He was in charge of the engine program? The engine parts would come from Pete Hutchinson and Keith Black to All American Racers and he would take them in a little windowless room and massage them. He was supposed to be working on the race engines. We're going along with the cars but nothing's happening with the engines—I don't hear engines running. We had our weekly meetings and I'd try to get a schedule and he wouldn't come up with anything. Dan would just make excuses and nothing happened.

One day, probably sometime in February, I just called up Pete

Hutchinson and I asked if Pete had any engines that I could use.

"What do you mean?" he asked. "We can't send you any engines; we're doing the Dodge engines. What about your engines?"

I explained to him what was happening. I said, "Look, if you want a car at Riverside to test in March, I gotta have an engine to put in that car right now."

He said he didn't have any race engines yet but he had a few development engines.

I told him I didn't care—just send me an engine. I suppose I should've gone to Dan and talked to him, but I didn't. I just went ahead and did what I did.

The KB truck shows up and starts to unload the engine from Keith Black and the phone rings. "Get up to the office!"

I go up to the office and they chew me out, Dan and Max Muhleman. I explained to them, I got this race car and we're doing good; the car's coming in on time, but I have to have an engine and I don't know what's going on over there in the engine shop. Plus, March is the test and in April we gotta be at Laguna Seca with two race cars, so I gotta have four engines. I don't have anything, not a peep. Nothing's turned over on the dyno, what are we gonna do?

They agreed and they decided to give me Jim Wright, who was a machine shop guy but liked to build engines and occasionally worked in the engine shop building engines. Ultimately, he became a very famous Indy engine guy; they put him in charge of our Trans Am race engine production.

We finally were able to get some stuff out of Miller and then he specced the rest of it. But Miller stayed in his little room building Dan's special engine, and we never heard from him, ever. I worked with Jim Wright, but I did use the engine that came from Pete's place because we had to. There was no time for anything else. We went testing at Riverside; Sam Posey came along with Dan and Swede Savage. I don't remember if they had a second driver yet for the Dodge, but he might have been there also. We tested the mule and they all drove the Plymouth.

<u>Time-Shift</u>—John Miller

John Miller was an obstacle but apparently he obstructed more them yours truly. Now this tale (rumor) was before my time but I have it on good authority that it is an authentic tale.What you would expect from the racer mindset? As I mentioned above, John had his private engine office/work space, behind closed doors with no widows to the outside world. He actually had a sign on the door that stated 'Engine Shop—Keep Out.' It was a small space but apparently it was his, and only his, space. As you might expect, this didn't sit too well with the chassis and car-build guys. One afternoon just before lunch, a number of shrewd individuals, who shall remain unspecified, procured a 4x8 sheet of plywood. With care and cunning they imprinted the words 'Chassis Shop—Keep Out' and placed it carefully against John's door and backed it up with the shop forklift! With that done, they depart for lunch. When John attempted to leave his lair, he was confronted by the new shop layout. Man against forklift, not a good bet. As fate would have it, Dan was still in his office when the call came through and was able to rescue the confined Miller. The plywood 'door' was deposed of and the fork lift returned to its stable, case closed. Life goes on.

SUSPENSION SNAFUS

THERE WERE MORE THAN a couple of things I had to do, so it was a very, very busy time. One of the first things Dan complained about when he saw what we had for a suspension layout was the so-called anti-dive and the associated caster change. With anti-dive, the upper control arm is skewed in the side view so that it provides the anti-dive capabilities, but an offshoot of that is you also have caster change. When the wheel moves up and down the caster changes so that when you're going into the turn, the caster's feedback changes, so it's going to vary as the wheel travels.

Dan said, "That's no good"—in stronger terms than that. "I wanna take that out."

That's a major job but we could do it. This is still in February before the test and we had a lot to do, but what the hell, it's only time. I had to design another set of control arms and I had to redesign the pivot points on the chassis. So the number one car, which is now the #42 car, still has that arrangement on it.

The conventional Chrysler car has an eccentric to adjust the caster and camber. The special control arms that I made for the test car were more like the Fords that had a dog bone with shims to adjust the caster and the camber. So I had to redesign the pivots; we had to be able to use both pickup points. We had to go and test A-B, B-A, back-to-back. I had to put these control arms in, take them out, then put the other control arms back in. The anti-dive was out of one configuration; we went from anti-dive to no dive with no caster change. We had anti-dive with caster change, no dive, no caster change.

I said, "This is no good, the car's gonna wander because the geometry will have a lot of scuff (lateral displacement of the tire with jounce and rebound)."

"It'll be okay," somebody said, but it twas't me.

I designed it, built all the pieces—special control arms, special steering arms and all that. This is all with my engine designer doing all the layout work, but I did pirate a little help. I would send all the data back to the Chrysler guys and they would run some computer stuff for me and they provided me with some of the pieces. That was kind of under the table because they weren't really supposed to be working on this 'outside' job. But I had friends at Chrysler and Pete in my corner. They were enthusiast guys, and it didn't take them very long to run that stuff.

On top of that I had one other extra, extra burden. I don't think I told this to anybody else, but Ray Caldwell was my cross to bear. Ray thought he was a car designer. He wanted some kind of a nightmare suspension incorporated into the Dodge. He wanted links on the rear suspension like he did on his Can-Am car, which in retrospect never worked on the Can-Am car. He made some sketches for me.

I looked at them and I said, "Well, guys, it's not gonna work with a leaf spring because the spring's gonna dictate the geometry and you wanna put these rods in there. It's gonna fight the geometry. The car will oversteer like crazy."

"No, no, no, we can do this and do that ..." Then they would say they could slot the front eyes for the springs ...

"Oh man, it's just not gonna work." I said to Hutch, "I'm not gonna build it."

He said, "Yeah, I think you're right. It's not gonna work but you gotta make them happy."

So I designed the stuff the way he wanted it and made all the pieces again so it would go in the Plymouth (there was no Dodge at this point).

We had all this stuff to test—a lot of work. The long and the short of it was that, yeah, the car darted all over the place and nobody liked the anti-dive suspension and they couldn't really pick up the feedback change with the caster change so they were happy with that. So we went back to the conventional front suspension—the anti-dive. There were some modifications to have a better camber curve and things like that, but essentially it was the anti-dive layout. When you take the anti-dive out you get lateral scuff—the tire scuffs, and under hard braking the car wants to dart around. You have more predictability with the anti-dive system. We went back to the conventional control arms, although we kept the dogbones and the shims because I didn't wanna go all the way back and go with eccentrics. The second car we built for Dodge and the second and three Plymouth cars we built were with the eccentrics.

So the #48 car that Craig Jackson owns has the eccentrics and the #42 car that Boone owns has the dogbones. The rear mods didn't work either; it was spinning out all over the place, so that came out and we went back to the leaf springs. Nobody said, "Good job, Bob." Life goes on.

BAD ACID TRIP

WE FINISHED THE CARS and the only thing with the Dodge was that, unbeknownst to us at the time, they didn't clean it up well after the acid-dipping and the body continued to etch. In particular, it was etching in the middle crossmember where the torsion bar anchors were. I think in our second race we were setting up a fix for that; we had to put some additional reinforcing rollbars in and weld them into the floor out in the field, and reinforce the floorpan. You could see it because you would adjust the car height and it would come back in sagging. It wouldn't maintain the car height because the torsion bars kept untwisting.

The Dodge had a particular bad go with that, for some reason Posey and Caldwell and those guys didn't want to fix it right away so they had more trouble with their Dodge than we had with the Plymouth. We put the fix in the Plymouth right away. They didn't fix the Dodge for another race or so. I don't really remember the details, but rumor has it that the Dodge also suffered from an undernourished roof. More than likely true because even with the Plymouths we had to be careful when leaning on the doors and roof. What a tangled web you weave when you practice to deceive.

I'M IN, I'M OUT AGAIN! THE LAYOFF

I THINK IN THE first four or five races we qualified on the pole like three times. For most people involved the Trans Am program was a failure because we never won a race, but to me it was one of the most successful projects I did because of the handicaps that we had. After about the 3rd or 4th race, Chrysler decided to pull out. They said, "We're cutting the budget in half and there will only be one car."

So Dan gave that car to Swede and we continued the year with Swede until the last two races, and then Dan decided he wanted to drive the last two races out of his own pocket. As we now know, apparently he had planned to retire after the last Riverside race.

The budget cut almost put me, personally, in the grease. It was a Friday night before the race (probably dark and stormy) ... this is one time my memory has let me down. I can't remember which race it was. Sorry bout that, but the facts of the event are all crystal clear.

After practice, a few of us had adjourned to the hotel lounge. Phil Remington (Rem) had flown in with a few other AAR guys, which in itself was unusual. The crew, myself and Swede have been in town since Thursday. I didn't have a clue.

One of the oddballs in attendance was a guy named Gary Wheeler, not my favorite person, we'll just leave it at that. He was pontificating to a couple of young gals at the bar about why he and Rem were in town. It seemed that there was a changing of the guard planned. To the point—I was getting the boot.

Rationale was complicated. Chrysler in all its wisdom and glory chopped the budget. Dan was forced to cut back to one car and was cutting me loose and popping Rem in my spot as team manager and race engineer; he was on their other payroll. Rem and I were discussing this in hushed tones at our table in the lounge. Dan wanted me home immediately, but I thought it wiser to wait until after the race on Sunday before making the announcement along with my exit. Less disturbance to the troops.

However, this clever, smooth transition was disrupted by the braggadocio at the bar. My two crew chefs, Bobby Box and Bert Brown overheard the nefarious plans and apparently decided on an alternate plan of their very own.

A short time after the 'leak' they came and sat down with Rem and me and flat out stated, "We understand you're leaving".

"Well yeah" I said, "but how the hell did you guys find out?"

They explained. Rem and I listened. Finally, Bobby and Bert said, "If they ask you to stay would you stay?"

I indicated that more than likely I would, but the exit plans were already in motion.

With huge smiles on their faces they told us that they had just called Max Muhleman and Dan Gurney and told them straight out. "If Tarozzi goes we all go," and so the tide was turned. AAR had little choice but to reinstate the lonely Turk warrior from Detroit. Sometimes bad things can end well.

Meanwhile Rem let out a sigh of relief. He was elated at not having to be on the road. At that time I hadn't realized all the travel time he had put in over the years, all the Shelby LeMans efforts, AAR IndyCar and Can-AM programs, as well as other shunts here and there. He mentioned a few of these but was reluctant to elaborate, so I never completely understood his hesitancy until many, many years later (see my Time–Shift Phil Remington insert above).

SHOWTIME!

THE NEXT-TO-THE-LAST RACE was Kent, Washington, and the last race was Riverside California, which is where Dan retired. He wanted to do those last two races, and AAR funded the completion of that third car because Swede had rolled the second car at Saint Jovite, Canada. I can't remember if we ever had the third car as a spare, probably so, but it raced for the first time at Kent. The new third car's number was #48 and Dan was driving it. It was the replacement for the original #42 car that Swede rolled. After Saint Jovite we just changed the numbers on the door and on the hood of the spare car, which was sitting in the truck carrying the #48. So the original #48 car became the #42 car, with a slight change in decals, and then Swede finished the year in that car. We actually ran a lot of races with just one car and no spare. That car has the most mileage, as a Trans Am car in the '70s, and then it continued to race a lot over the years in SCCA Historical races.

WHERE THE RUBBER LEAVES THE ROAD ... AND SO DO I

THE FINAL RACE, RIVERSIDE California. Dan was back in car #48 and Swede in old faithful #42. We're doing battle with the mighty FoMoCo Mustang and as usual we're a little behind. All season long Swede had felt that we were at a disadvantage with the Goodyear tires. He felt that the Firestones were just better and was one of the factors that put the Fords ahead of us. I can't remember who suggested it first, but the subject of trying the Firestones on the Plymouth came up in our conversations.

I asked, "Are you sure, Swede?"

He said he was.

That's all I needed to hear; I was off and running on a new mission (biting the hand that was feeding me—again). I called over to Bobby Box, my main crew chief and accomplisher of all things devious, and had him ease on over to the Firestone tent and mount up a set of tires. Swede had previously arranged this clandestine operation with the Firestone guys. Now, mind you, this is not some midnight operation. This is in the middle of qualifying in front of God and everybody.

As we are mounting the tires on the car, the Goodyear rep comes over to me and goes ballistic. Many expletives were exchanged; he says I can't, especially here.

I say I can, and I am, and he storms off.

Cut to the chase, the car goes approximately one-half second quicker on the Firestones. And that was without any suspension changes or adjustments. Swede and I put our heads together and decide on educated guesses as to the necessary changes to be made, and I cast the order to the crew. In retrospect, we should have consulted with Dan G, but what the hell, we just wanted to win and were blind as to any nebulous concept of chain of command.

Showdown in the desert. The next morning proved to be a different story. Swede approached me in the garage and said that we had been summoned to a meeting in the race truck with Dan. Not a good way to start the day. Dan talked primarily to Swede and essentially stated that even though Swede did not have a specific contract with Goodyear, if he wanted to have a future with AAR, and specifically in Indy Cars, he would not run the Firestone tires. Not a command, just a 'suggestion.' I don't believe I was spoken to at any time during the discussion. I now know that my fate had already been decided.

We returned the car to its previous setup with the Goodyears, no easy job on the morning of the race, and ran the race as best we could. The race was won by Parnelli Jones in the Mustang. We finished fourth and fifth, Swede and Dan. We did a decent job considering the traumatic events that developed during the race. But nobody and I mean nobody, was going to best Jones. He drove like a man possessed and was a joy to watch. My hat off to you, PJ.

With my fate sealed and 'don't let the door hit you in the butt on the way out' at AAR, I was off to my next adventure.

But first I must clear up the record as best as I can. This isn't easy, but I'll have a go. Dan and I never did get along really well. It's complicated, egos always are. Let's face it, I was a pushy kid who leaped before he looked (but I always trusted my cape!). I always had this grandiose idea that the team manager/race engineer ran the show. In retrospect, I was wrong. Dan and I had a few early clashes. The most obvious clash was the test car engine episode, not so delicately handled by yours truly and outlined above. There were a few other minor incidents as the year progressed. The big showdown happened at Riverside after the major insubordinate move with Firestone tires. See, they're starting to add up aren't they.

It's race time and we are about ten to fifteen laps into the race. Swede came in for his first full stop, a little early but nevertheless, there he was. We had planned a right front tire change only, along with the fuel. I'm patiently waiting for the fueler to finish when one of the Goodyear reps taps me on the shoulder and indicates that the two rear tires needed to be changed. My only non-command verbal response was, "Holy shit."

I grabbed Bobby and Bert" told them what needed to be done and without a moment's hesitation they were on the jacks. We never had considered that we would have to change two rear tires at the same time. We had never tested the jack points for such a scenario.

But clever dudes that they were, Bobby and Bert carefully raised the back of the car from the two opposed jack points, left and right, while I even more carefully attempted to keep the car from rocking on the two jack points. It worked! The tires where changed and the Swede left the pits with very little time lost over our planned stop for fuel. Not two seconds mind you, but probably a record for such a bizarre stop.

Now came crunch time. The two rear tires were shredded down to the cords, both of them. My instant response was to get out the pit board and call Dan in. T'was before headsets, you see. I'm sure Dan saw the board but he kept on trucking. Finally after several additional laps he came into the pits and we proceeded to change the two rear tires as well as refuel the car.

Dan is yelling and screaming at me. I really couldn't hear him but I finally got the point. I apparently was able to brief him regarding the rear tire predicament. His response to me was, essentially, I'm Dan Gurney and I don't f*****g burn down rear tires. Nevertheless, there we were.

Another rather excellent pit stop, despite the conditions, and Dan was back out on the track. Now comes the bad part; the tires were pristine. Dan was absolutely correct—he doesn't burn down rear tires, especially at Riverside. Well, shit in my hat. But wait, it's not over. Having gone only one lap, Dan pulls back into the pits with the front spoiler broken in two pieces. We immediately trim it back and send him back out. Don't ask me why we didn't have a spare spoiler with a couple of Dzus fasteners; we just didn't.

So as I stated above, we finished fourth and fifth, Swede and Dan. But wait, it's still not over. Dan pulls into the pits and reads me the riot act, reiterating the points outlined above. I listen, but not for long. I carefully point out that he should be praising the crew and me, of course, for an outstanding intuitive performance we produced virtually under the gun, and in front of god and everybody. My last 'parting' point was that if he hadn't lost his cool, charged out onto the track, ripped the spoiler off, which precipitated a return to the pits, he would have finished at least a position or two farther towards the front. And with that, I walked away and, I guess out.

Unofficially I assumed that I had been let go by All American Racers after our debacle at the race. Bright and early Monday morning, when the adrenalin subsided and everyone had regained their composure, Dan Gurney offered me a job on the Indy Car program. But I didn't think—in fact, I knew—I couldn't get along with John Miller, Dan's resident engine wizard, and so I decided to walk. Where to, I knew not. (As I look back I think I jumped off the ship a little too soon, but maybe not. You be the judge.)

7

BIRTH OF THE KEITH BLACK ALUMINUM HEMI BLOCK

It's now late 1970 and I was sort of in limbo. I started to surf, race bicycles, anything with competition. For me that was primo. I and contemplated the universe, wondering what my next move would be. Liz and the kids were with me in California; I had no job, but life was good. After all, it was December back in Detroit. It now seems, in retrospect, that this turned out to be a very definitive time period in my life. As Yogi Berra said, "If you come to a fork in the road, take it." I took the fork but I knew not why. As I look back, it was the most significant change I'd made in my life, because at this point I think I deserted my dream, my longtime dream of being a race car driver. I didn't really realize it at that time, but now as I glance over my shoulder, that was the case.

Suddenly it was 1971, and a phone call came in from my old boss and friend Tom Hoover. We chatted for a while and then Tom asked me what my plans were. Actually, I didn't have any, but I'm sure I did a little tap dance around the subject. Finally, Tom asked if I might have some time to evaluate a new cylinder head that they were developing for drag racing. What else would Tom have his fingers in? The work would be done at Keith Black's shop in Southgate, California, just a short drive from where I lived in Huntington Beach.

Now you have to understand, with the exception of numerous engine builds and racing activities as a young lad back in good old New England, most of my engineering education and work experience was related to suspension, chassis work and race development. My formal engine development work was limited to a stint in the development lab at Chrysler. Mind you, I had a feel for engines—AMX drag race engine design and development, Javelin

NASCAR design and development. Well maybe I did know a little bit about engines, but I wasn't sure that Tom knew what I knew (or didn't know).

WESTLAKE WONDER

As it turned out, Chrysler had contracted with Harry Westlake, English engine wizard, to design a new version of the Hemi cylinder head. Chrysler's subversive designation was D5. The engine lab at Chrysler had run the head but the valve guides kept falling out and they didn't really want to spend any time on a redesign. I think it was the old 'not invented here' syndrome. So I agreed to have a look and see what I could do. Little did I know what that little project would lead to in the years to come.

From that little seedling of a project, I managed to realize ten years of engine design and development programs from Chrysler. For ten years I did all, and I emphasize all, of Chrysler's race engine work. Drag race, road race, rally, off road and NASCAR. From the Mitsubishi 2-liter motor to the stroked Hemis and 440s. Later I expanded into basic R&D of turbocharging a selection of Chrysler production engines. You name it, I did it. I did the design work, oversaw the buildups, and ran the dyno on a daily basis. What a gig!

THE KEITH BLACK ALUMINUM HEMI

One day, early in the game, I was called into Keith Black's office. Yeah, I had a little office of my own there at the KBRE works, all 80 square feet—an 8x10 closet, I think. Anyhow, I sat down with KB and Holly Hedrick, KB's sales manager and man-in-the-field.

KB says, "Well, Turk,, do you think you could design an aluminum Hemi block for Top Fuel and Funny Car application?"

"Sure," says I. Now think about it for a minute: this is normally a job for a team of designers and engineers, and at that time Top Fuel engines were making somewhere between 4000 to 5000 horsepower using cast-iron blocks, material they made anchors from. And if I recall correctly, I had never been inside a foundry before.

All that was about to change. KB was worried that he might not sell enough blocks to pay for all the costs involved. KB was a worrier like that. Holly, on the other hand, was ever the optimist. "No problem," he says, "I'll sell every one you can put out the door."

Of course, there was a little more to the story. At that time Chrysler was out of cast-iron Hemi blocks and they were not going to make any more because they had 'lost' the tooling. Go figure. So the real decision for the aftermarket folks was whether to manufacture the new version of the Hemi from cast iron or aluminum. For us it was a no-brainer; aluminum was the flavor of choice. The real question, of course, was would it be strong enough. You all know the answer—just look out the window and down the strip. But it wasn't easy, believe me, but that's a story for another day.

What the hell, I'll tell it now. My 'design' approach at this time was not what you would call standard operating procedure. To expedite the process, and of course this was way before CAD modeling was on the scene, I obtained the block paper drawings from Chrysler and marked them up in red. I added a few sections here and there and I was ready to go. KB and I shopped around for a pattern shop that might be capable of undertaking this job. We ended up at a rather large facility nearby and were assigned a pattern maker by the name of Swede Renberg. Funny how some names stick with you. In any event, due to my minimal drawing approach, I spent many hours in the pattern shop pointing and changing as we went along. Suddenly we had the cores completed and were in the foundry.

Foundries are hellish places, complete with fire and brimstone. We suffered a lot but we learned a lot, especially me, because I spent a lot of time in the heat and smoke. Getting good quality casting on a consistent basis was always a problem. Then one day our savior walked right in the front door.

I got a call from KB's receptionist about a guy who wanted to see KB but KB was busy. Would I take to him? Sure. He was a fan of drag racing and he wanted to meet KB, but, a big but, he also happen to be in charge of Alcoa's R&D facilities in Pennsylvania. Somewhere in the conversation he asked if we might be interested in Alcoa producing KB's block at their R&D facilities. He then invited us to visit the facilities and see what might be done. Now, strictly speaking the R&D facilities were normally limited to producing one or two, maybe a dozen, prototype items. But when you're the boss you can call the shots, and he was and he did. I learned more about casting than I ever imaged. Pattern techniques, chill types and placement and the how's, whys and timing of effective heat treatment. For the time being there was nary a bad casting in sight.

Meanwhile, back to our earlier reality and dilemma. The first block had been made. It was out of the foundry and through the machining process and hanging on an engine stand in KB's engine shop. And there it hung for many weeks, even months, as I recall. KB was thinking, and thinking, and contemplating his next move. We all knew that testing was the next logical step but it was a huge one.

Stage right, enter Candies and Hughes, drag racers personified. "Okay KB, it's time to get off your ass. We need this aluminum block. We're getting desperate. Tell you what we're going to do. We will supply all the parts and pieces to build the engine as well as our dragster and driver. Let's go test that creation of yours."

A deal like that was impossible to pass up. KB agreed and Holly was jumping for joy. Well, not exactly jumping. If you knew Holly, you'd know he was gravitationally challenged.

HEMI HAMMERING

THE ENGINE WAS ASSEMBLED by Mike Snively who played a dual role here. He was an engine tech at KB's shop, assigned to me to work on the various Chrysler projects. He also just happened to be C&H's driver at the time. Mike was assigned to me because no one else at KB's could get along with him, so they gave him to the new guy. Mike and I got along just fine, although it was verbal barbs and arrows all the time. You gotta think that after driving a Top Fuel car on the weekend at a mere 250 mph, screwing together gasoline development engines would be pretty mundane and boring. But he jumped into this project with both feet—a free motor and a paid ride.

The Day of Reckoning. Place: Irwindale dragstrip. Time: mid-morning on a sunny Southern California day. First thing out of Leonard Hughes' mouth, in his thick Southern drawl was a shot at KB. "Y'all see that amb'lance over there? That's not for Mike. That's for KB when he falls over with a heart attack after the first pass."

Little did he know what lay ahead, or maybe he did? No heart attack but symptoms thereof. The first pass was slow and easy, probably under 200 mph. Immediately, and I mean like on our way down the track to pick up the dragster and tow it back to the pits, KB proclaims that that was good enough. "Let's go back to the shop so we can look at it while it's still in one piece." That's what a designer lives for: confidence in his creation.

To a man, with the exception of KB, we announce,"No way, we stay."

KB relented, we stayed. To shorten a protracted story, we made approximately a half dozen passes, inching our way up to a little better than 225 mph, or thereabouts. Time has a way of dulling the memory, usually for the better. Remember, the older I get, the better I was. Anyway, late afternoon, last pass. Tip the can and open the throttle was the order of the moment. The smoke was just starting to clear and the dragster was approaching the first light. BAA-BOOM-OH, sputter-sputter.

KB almost falls to earth but we all brace him up and suggest we travel the 1320 and see what's what. As we approach the shutdown area, we spot Snively standing next to the dragster holding one of the magnetos and waving it triumphantly in the air. Just a misfire, KB, just a misfire. There was joy in Mudville this day, the mighty KB had not struck out. As time would show the world, the mighty KB had hit a home run with a little help from his friends.

DYNO DYNAMICS

UNLESS YOU'VE BEEN THERE, done that, and collected a tee shirt or two, you wouldn't have any idea as to the brutal punishment an engine undergoes on the dyno. Drag race engines were special when it came to dyno testing. They are a somewhat delicate engine, built with minimum clearances and fragile components. After all, they only have to use WOT for a matter of seconds. So we tended to treat them a little like prima donnas. Today it's even worse, with accelerated runs. What wimps. Back in the day, a dyno run was done with gusto. Open the throttle, wide now, open wide at an RPM just below the peak torque and hold it there until you collect the data. Now, remember this was BC (before computers). I was lucky if I had one or two data collectors (of the human type) with pencil and paper. They would each write down the data points they were assigned.

I would maintain the engine RPM by manipulating the brake control (that's Heenan dyno talk for the water valve) and also read the torque output. When everyone was done, I would breathe the engine a bit by partially closing the throttle and loosen up the controller for the next RPM point, about plus 400 RPM. Then wide open again, dial in the RPM and collect the data. This usually took about 10 to 15 seconds, sometimes 20 if it was a particularly unstable point. I would continue up to just over peak engine speed and then back down in the 400 RPM steps. The engine blowby was our absolute guide in matters of engine condition, usually 1.5 to 3.0 cubic feet per minute. Over that and off it came from the dyno, strap on the backup engine, re-establish a baseline and continue on down the road.

We always had a spare engine of whatever in the engine room. Blowby was my absolute criterion for the basic condition of the engine. Tom Hoover adopted this rule to the point where he would be at the drag races and go around with his six-inch rule measuring the height that each racer's breather caps had lifted off the valve cover. If it was over X he would suggest that they change engines or change their engine builder. Not very scientific but it was Tom's way and worth a few laughs.

Laughs are good, but working at this level requires a lot of focus and concentration and maybe a little skill. I can't speak for everyone, but when I design a part, or a complete engine for that matter, or run an engine on the dyno at the level I'm speaking of here, I have to get inside. I get right inside the engine, see and feel the piston and valve movements, feel the pulses and vibrations. It's not unlike driving a race car or motorcycle at 10/10ths. You focus, focus, and then focus some more. Which reminds me—you had to know this was coming—of an incident while running one of the 396 drag race Hemis on the dyno.

On this occasion my 'helper' was Stan Shiroma. For those of you who are nostalgically challenged, on the weekends Stan was the driver of a top Funny Car called the Midnight Skulker, which he co-owned with Ray Zeller another 'helper' at KB's. I had quite a selection of talent, believe me. Halfway through the dyno run, I felt a slight tremor in the floor which, in turn, set my intestines to vibrating in sympathy. I instinctively eased the throttle back and shut down the motor. Stan, who was no slouch in these matters, was puzzled, to say the least. I told Stan to pull the motor off the dyno and that we would do a full inspection. Something just didn't feel right.

After we disassembled the engine, we found that one of the intake valves had a segment cracked about 90 percent across, to within one-eight inch from both edges of the valve. You had to see it to believe it (visual proof is located in the photos section of the book). The delicately-precarious positioning of that segment was surreal. Was it skill or luck? I'll let you be the judge. The next day Stan presented me with a 'trophy,' a wooden plaque with the valve mounted at the appropriate angle. The attached copper plate read:"Fastest Throttle—Bob Tarozzi." That trophy still has a prominent place on my office desk.

NASCAR and Trans-Am engines were a different breed. Sort of like a man's man among engines. Again, WOT just below the torque peak and start collecting data. When all the data was collected for that point, I would adjust the brake controller and move on to the next RPM point. No breathing of the engine this time. Up to peak power and then back down to just under peak torque in 400 RPM increments. Usually I would repeat this sequence three times to get sets of data for each RPM point to give me a valid average. All in the day of the life of a real race engine.

One time we were testing a 305 LA-engine destened for NASCAR when the winged cars were no longer allowed to run the Hemi. The engine was to run on a NASCAR oval track somewhere in the Deep South; I believe it is referred to as 'Daytona.' We had calculated the fuel consumption between pit stops and designated the number of tanks of fuel, as well as the number of pit stops required. The Chrysler wizards had also calculated the amount of engine speed that would be lost because of tire scuff in the turns.

With all this info in hand, the throttle was opened. It stayed there while the engine speed was varied with the dyno brake controller to simulate the actual engine speed changes in the turn, somewhere in the neighborhood of 500 RPM. When it came time for our 'pit stop,' the throttle was closed to idle and remained there for the length of the pit stop. After the pit stop, it was back out on the 'track.' This was repeated until the end of the race, which we won! On the dyno it's easy to win. We ran on into the night and were honored with a few visits from the local constabulary. Fortunately they were fans; that KB was a charmer.

TAKIN' IT TO THE TRACK

AFTER THE TROPHIES WERE 'handed out', two engines were built and shipped to Mario Rossi's NASCAR team and installed in a 1971 winged Dodge Daytona. Richard Brooks drove the Dodge to a third place finish in the Daytona 500 Qualifier. He led the 500 for five or more laps at various times during the race and eventually finished seventh after a crash resulted in a lengthy pit stop. Not bad for an engine the size of a lunch box—so said Richard Brooks.

The ubiquitous Chrysler 273/318 cubic inch LA-series engine had a lot of lives. First it bulked up into a 330-cube alcohol burning Indy engine. Then it went on an extreme diet and came out as the Trans-Am 305-inch package, then the short-lived NASCAR 'lunch box.' Next we added fuel injection and a dry sump and—Shazam!, it appears in open-wheeled missiles. And let us not forget the 340 and the many other drag race combinations. It also spawned a cousin in the form of the 360-inch truck motor. Cast crank and all, it became an effective power plant for numerous off-road rides. I'm sure I forgot somebody, but nevertheless it had a good life.

8 OIL PANS, MANIFOLDS, TURBOCHARGERS .... AND THE AX!

It was now about the mid-'70s and Chrysler projects were coming fast and furious. Shepherding the KB alloy Hemi block was practically a full-time job in itself. Again the phone rings. I love it when the phone rings! In my business, if the phone rings you answer it.

DRY SUMP BOOGIE

"Dry sumps you say, sure, why does it work, I don't really know, let's find out? OK, how do we do that? Do whatever it takes. OK, Tom, talk to you in a few weeks."

Conversation between Tom Hoover and me on the eve of an adventurous indulgence into the oily depths of high speed, normally aspirated, reciprocating, spark ignition engines. Amen. This was typical Tom Hoover, the best boss anyone could ever have. He would plant an idea, then cut you loose and let you run with it. He would never look over my shoulder or barrage me with his presence. He came to California every month or so, more to visit sunny California than to check on me or the project. My reports and phone calls were sufficient to track the progress of the project, but he liked to visit and chat. And I do believe that he was a bit jealous that he didn't have the opportunity to get his hands dirty back in Detroit, what with labor unions and all.

The dry sump program expanded beyond our wildest visions. First, it was how deep should the pan be? OK, let's build one-inch spacers and keep adding and subtracting until something bad, or good, happens. Well, that was interesting. Now, what about the shape of the pan? Dozens of pan shapes littered the dyno room floor before we found an answer. And I say 'an' answer because the first thing you learn in development work is that you never have 'the' answer, only 'an' answer, until the next one comes along. Oh, and which side should the pickups be on, left or right? Good question. Windage tray? Sure, why not? Finally came the pump and the all-mighty question of how many stages. This task started out rather simply. Establish a given pressure pump size and then add a few suction stages of equal capacity each. Sounded simple until the dyno sheets poured forth.

Every time I added a suction stage, the power increased. Two stages, three, four, five, six, what the hell, is there no end? Finally practicality reared its ugly head. No one would want, or could fit, a six- or seven-stage pump into their race car. Maybe we could use larger lines with fewer stages? Same answer. Started with —10 lines and got up to —16 lines, even with six stages. A Hydra of my own creation was born right there in Southgate, California. Again practicality won the day and four suction stages with —12 lines became the oiling platform of choice.

You might be wondering—if this was such a good deal how come my Dragster and Funny Car buddies didn't use them? Here is where old man practicality comes into the picture again. Top Fuel engines are really fragile monsters and when they hiccup they create a lot of little bits and pieces which make their way into the oiling system. No way to 'clean up' between rounds so the complete system would have to be changed—not practical. I had to agree. So we parted friends. There were plenty of other eager souls waiting with open crankcases.

> <u>Time–Shift</u>—*Dry Sump Update*
> *As many of you now know, dry sump systems have made their way into the Funny Car field, ostensibly for 'safety,' but they're there and they're working. I wish I knew exactly why, but after all I am a bit out of touch. I have asked, but gotten no meaningful responses. However, that doesn't keep me from pontificating and speculating on this seemingly controversial subject.*

Although the current Funny Car application is a far cry from what a dry sump system should be, it's a start. As I understand it, they are only using one stage of suction. Yeah, one stage, not six or eight. It appears they just don't understand. A good friend of mine once said that if their tow truck broke down they would have to call AAA to get it started. Got it. (That was him talkin, not me.) They have improved the bearing life slightly, if at all. The real problem is the life of the crankshaft, six to eight runs. The loads are horrendous, and then some. Fuel quantities and blower pressure continue to rise and they continually creep up on the engine speed. It's a lose-lose situation. Such is life in the fast lane. The bottom line is that it seems to be 'working,' limited as it is and the dragsters are following suit. Got to mean somethin'.

MANIFOLD MAZE

MANIFOLDS AND CAMSHAFTS were consumed in large quantities. I received various manifold configurations from all the aftermarket manufacturers and I created many of them myself, although I recall that manifold creations were one of T. Hoover's pet projects.

We made some by cutting and pasting existing manifolds; others were hammered completely from sheet aluminum. Those were works of art. Popsicle sticks—my tools of choice for taming the monster plenum manifolds that had a mind of their own when it came to fuel distribution. Glue them in, move them here, then turn them this way and that.

Camshafts were run by the dozens. In and out in 30 minutes advanced a bit, retarded a bit. Next! Sometimes they all blurred together. And then after I picked a few that looked promising they still had to be run in a car. The times at the track were the ultimate evaluator. The Timex tells the tale.

If you think about it for more than a millisecond, you realize that the fuel/air mixture has a mass, and a typical race car supplies a significant acceleration to that mass when it moves up or around the track. $F=MA$: you all remember that, I'm sure. The resulting force moves the fuel/air mixture to the side or rear, or just around and around. Bad deal. The dyno results give the tuner a goal, something to shoot for. It requires a lot of tender loving care to even come close to that goal. That's where a good tuner earns his wages, little as they are.

Carburetted manifolds pointed us to fuel injection, which turned my thinking upside down for just a brief moment in time. The mystery appeared in the form of an IR (individual runner) manifold for the Hemi. An individual runner intake manifold places each throat of the carburettor directly over the intake runner. Sort of a one-on-one setup. In most cases, the carburettors are located as an extension of the intake runner. In other cases, the carburettors are placed directly over the intake runner but with a plenum in between. You could look at this setup as a pseudo fuel injection. Pretty close, especially if you remove the plenum. But here's the bump—the FI made less power!

I had run into an illogical distortion of reality. FI is just supposed to be better, right? Well, wrong, at least for now. Once I got this paradox lodged in my brain, I couldn't rest until I had an answer. It took several engines—wore them out, you see—and many assaults on the current logic, along with numerous cuts and tries, and the answer was as simple as could be. The main difference between the two systems was that the carbs let the fuel in way up high in the inlet tract, whereas the conventional FI, at the time, dropped the fuel in down low. Some were even proud of the fact that they could squirt right in on the valve.

With this bit of deduction in hand, I began to raise the injector nozzles up in the runner body. I wouldn't bore you with all the combinations and permutations. The final magic number was four inches from the top of the trumpet opening, circa 1975. There is really no magic in the universe of engine tuning. My number at that time and place was four inches based on minimizing the standoff, and accompanying power and fuel economy losses. But let us not forget the effects of intake runner length, camshaft overlap and exhaust lengths, among other things. Keeping this all in mind you need to move the nozzles as high as possible without losing out to the foggy standoff. Oh, would you like to know the reason behind this phenomenon? Cooling.

I'll let you work out the details.

> <u>Time–Shift</u>—*FI Update*
> *Circa 2013 (talk about time warp!): Formula One gurus now squirt the fuel in form above the trumpet, with impressive pressure, I assume! Wish I was still there!*

CHEVY ROCKERS ANYONE?

SOMETIMES YOU JUST GOTTA punt. Another one of those phone calls from T. Hoover: "What's happening, kid? If you're not too 'busy' I got a little task for you." Apparently, one the 'guys' had an epiphany. This gentleman will remain anonymous, except to say he was a gentleman farmer from Ohio. Anyway, in this dream the Chevy "floppy" rocker gear was graphed onto the Mopar small-block and the revs soared.

My reaction was unprintable, and I did rant on for a while. The Mopar engines have an envious shaft arrangement with nicely defined rigid rocker arms. Now, in the beginning there were some oiling issues but those had been solved. The Chevy rocker arrangement was the way it was because it was extremely cheap to make for production, but it was barely serviceable for racing. It is light but not stable at speed. Hoover wanted me to design the pseudo rocker, build it and test it at KB's.

We debated at length. Finally, I caved and agreed to design and build it, but the testing had to be done back in Detroit on their valve fixture at Teddy Spehar's facilities. That way when it failed—when, not if—I would be innocent of any wrongdoing.

As suspected, valve float occurred sooner with the Chevy floppers than with the standard Mopar shaft rockers. Amen to that. And think about it for a second: Where have all the aftermarket rocker manufacturers gone for their high-speed packages? You know it—shafts my friend, shafts. Yet another set of left turns to get back where we started.

INTAKE ACTION

Now, just so you don't leave with the impression that I always did the right thing, read on. Even the tall can be small. It was somewhere around 1976 when I met Paul Rossi at the World Finals in Ontario, California. He was a contract racer, sort of. He got parts and pieces but little else from Chrysler. In spite of that handicap, he did amazingly well in Super Stock with his Hemi-powered Plymouth.

t seems he had come up with a scheme to trick the power curve. It was quite simple but effective. At that time, the Hemi Superstocks were using the bathtub intake manifold. It looked like it sounded. A huge empty space plenum, located between the carburettor and the inlet runners on their way to the intake port. With the lid off, it looked like a bathtub. The carbs were perched on top of all this mess.

Essentially, the plenum was meant to fool the engine into thinking that it had a monster carburettor to draw from. It worked and picked up the top-end power and was good for a top-end speed advantage. However, it produced holes in the torque curve at the lower RPM. Not the best thing for launching and grabbing those race-winning ETs.

Paul came up with a clever workaround to get the best of both worlds. A simple flapper valve mounted inside the plenum which was operated by a vacuum valve, essentially changing the volume over a short time period—possibly the world's first active intake manifold.

Hoover liked, it but wanted to know more about how and why it worked. He hooked me up with Paul and we spent a day on the dyno. But alas, try as I might I could not find the reason why. Remember now, we were still using a static testing procedure, steady state on the dyno, and as it turns out, the flapper valve mechanism is dynamic.

With some short-sightedness, I pronounced the idea just a maybe, without much enthusiasm as I recall. Paul continued to win and somebody out there was watching and listening because, if you look closely, most of the production high-performance engines today have variable intake plenums and runners. Velocity is the name of the game. Thumbs up for Paul, the gong and hook for the Turk.

There were lots of other projects, both sanctioned and unsanctioned by the boys in Detroit—make that Highland Park, but nevertheless blessed by Pope Tom. off-road engine and vehicle development with John Baker, Bill Stroppe and Walker Evans. I even rode shotgun for a series of desert events with John Baker in his two-wheel-drive Dodge truck. The Stroppe-built Dodge Ramchargers made it to the African Safari Rally with Malcolm Smith at the wheel. Yeah, that Malcolm Smith. He could read the desert like he had built-in radar.

Then there were two FI 305 road racing engine development projects: one as a 'sponsor' and race engineer for a Swede Savage entry in the 1972 Questor Formula One inaugural race at Ontario Motor Speedway, the other a year-long engine development program in conjunction with UOP Shadow Formula 5000, circa 1975.

There; I have logged in the details of the multifaceted lives of the Mopar small block which will always remain dear to my heart, in spite of my fathering of the aluminum block Hemi fuel motor.

TURBO TIME

PRODUCTION ANYONE? ERA—circa 1976. This time it was a conference call from T. Hoover and Bob Cahill, the man himself. It seems that they were interested in turbocharging production engines but the production engineering group was not. So how would I like to add this to my résumé—basic R&D into the turbocharging of production engines.

Sure, why not? At this point in time, only the Japanese thought this had any merit. This was a very complicated adventure. But the bottom line was that I had to move north to team up with the UOP Shadow works, where they had two dynamometers. This would allow me to continue the race engine development as well as delve into the world of turbocharging the Chrysler line of engines: slant-six, small-block V8, and four-cylinder Mitsubishi.

Everything had to be designed and built from scratch, because nothing existed. I developed an instrumentation system that could look into the cylinder while it was running. I was taking photos of the combustion process and watching detonation begin its destructive process. Who woulda thunk? I built and developed a turbocharged package for the 225 slant-six, 318 V8, and two-liter Mitsubishi four-cylinder. I stuffed them into vehicles and shipped them back to Detroit, where they disappeared into the bowels of the 'not invented here' department. The resulting report was huge, dyno runs, pressure traces, and photos galore, but I doubt it was ever read by anybody but Hoover and Cahill.

To give you a glimpse into the kind of confidence Hoover had in yours truly, get a hold of this. The slant-six turbo package was stuffed into a pickup truck. Tom came to Marina, the Shadow subsidiary, to have a firsthand look at all the delightful packages we had amassed. The pickup was the only vehicle we had running at the moment. He drove it around the Monterey Peninsula for about a day or two and then announced that he was headed back to Detroit. I don't know if he had Triple A or Triple B(alls), but he was out of there. I think he had a racers heart—stick your foot in it and steer. He made it back without a hiccup. The pickup was eventually parked alongside the V8 van and the Mitsubishi whatever, where they all slowly turned to rust.

Curiosity! Of course, as always, I could not help but wonder what was happening inside the race engines. You'll remember, I hope, that I had developed an instrumentation package for the turbo project that could view what was happening inside the cylinder while the engine was running and under load. So I hooked up one of my Hemi patients to the oscilloscope and recorded its lifelines as well. It looked like a heart surgery operating room, just not quite as sanitary. The results staggered the imagination. It was a world that few had seen before. I recorded and analyzed the results. Tom and I discussed the meaning of life inside the combustion chamber, but our time on earth together was fortuitously shortened.

END OF THE LINE

Whoa, what a ride! I thought it would never end, but end it did. Fast forward to 1979. Lee Iacocca comes on board and decides that, in an effort to save the company he would cut the majority of outside programs. Guess what? Race engine development work in California was not high on the protected species list. The ax came down; I was instructed to fold my tent and ship various parts and pieces to the chosen few who had survived the bloodletting.

With a foggy head, I for once in my life did what I was told without asking any stinging questions. Big mistake! I have often been asked if I knew at the time I was involved in any of these various projects that they would be so successful or lasting. Hell no! If I knew that, I would have stashed some of the cars or engines, even photographs or whatever and I would be a millionaire collector peddling my wares on eBay. Who knew, certainly not me, not single-minded, narrow-visioned Bob Tarozzi.

Believe it, my friends; there was a time when individualism was a positive and meaningful pursuit. Unlike today, where you must be part of a team and play by the rules, whatever that means. Thankfully, I am from the former time and place. For all who missed that moment in time, I have attempted to take you back where an individual was able to pursue a course to his liking, wear a multitude of hats and shift gears at a moment's notice without losing momentum.

Eventually, I found that I was in danger of losing my hats in the whirlwind. I hung in there as long as I could, always taking on projects that circumvented the system. Once a rebel—always a rebel, although I like to think of myself as a rebel with a cause. I guess I just enjoyed doing what people said I could not do! RESIST CONVENTIONAL WISDOM and REBEL WITH CAUSE. But eventually, the system won. Why should someone hire me to design a complex part when they could hire a selection of in-house guys to do their bidding?

This might sound bitter, but it's not. The racing business was good to me and I learned a lot. It provided huge challenges, much satisfaction, some tears, and many lasting friendships. What it did not provide was money. Racing is a 24/7 occupation with very little pay. So for those out there who would consider racing as a career, be aware of the commitment required and the twisted perception of rewards. Regrets? I've had a few, but then again, too few to mention. I did what I had to do and saw it through without exemption. I did it my way!

Thanks Frank S, Tom H, Larry R, Peter H, and KB.

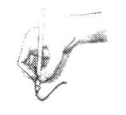

Part Three

The After Years

9 LEGAL DETOUR

WELL, HERE I AM AT another crossroad. Just barely moved to Carmel Valley, California, and the future (what future?) has evaporated. I just had the rug pulled out from underneath me. Chrysler pulled out and put me on the deck and I've got to get back up. Lee Iacocca, bless his little old heart, has come on board and declared war on outside contractors, one of whom was your's truly. Three choices: move back to Detroit, move back to Southern Cal, where most of the work was, or stay here in Carmel Valley. From a location standpoint, it's a no-brainer but from an economics standpoint it required a little thought.

Now begins the trek through the after years of the mind and the soul. Myths, Mad Schemes, Sagas, Fables, Folk and Fairy Tales, and some Truths.

Once again, I traveled to the magical land of Southern California to seek out friends and opportunities. After bouncing around among the usual suspects, I touched base with an old Chrysler buddy, Jon McKibben. He had toiled for a number of years in the road test garage back at the works. He then moved to Southern California and began applying his trade and talents of car testing to the yet infant vehicle crash testing field. He also connected with the fledging organization referred to as NHTSA (National Highway and Traffic Safety Administration). From there he migrated into the newly formed group of litigation orientated automotive engineers referred to as 'expert witnesses' (their term not mine). Okay, enough background—you can see were this is going.

Jon was up to his ears with work. Cut to the chase he hired me to conduct some lab tests at his shop. Simple stuff like construct a test buck for loading and ultimately failing car seats. A test fixture for evaluating the failure modes of the infamous Ford Park-to-Reverse problems, etc. Now, this was just part time work so I would fly back and forth between Carmel Valley and Santa Ana California once, sometime twice a week. Point of interest—the airlines were still being subsidized by the Federales and flights were fifty or sixty bucks. After a while I ended up buying a marginal Plymouth Horizon and parked it at LAX. Rent-a-cars can drain your pocket pretty quickly.

After a while Jon started towing me around with him and introducing me to a number of his law firm clients. This led to a few uncomplicated cases for me to implement on my own. Nothing like jumping straight into the deep end of the pool after learning a few basic strokes. You struggle, you gasp for air, you either sink or swim, or you learn to float on top. Floating isn't fun, but it gets you to shore. One day while I was recovering on shore I got THE call. Another one of those fortuitous occurrences of life which are unexplainable but welcomed with open arms.

The bad news: Jon was a motorcycle racer, and in a race at Riverside, California he crashed—big time. As a result he was 'temporarily' a quadriplegic. At the time of the incident 'temporary' was not in the equation and Jon was constrained with clamps and screws and lots of tubes. He was alert and surprisingly talkative and confident of his recovery. But (this is the good news for me), he was due to testify in Detroit in a few weeks. He wanted to plug me into the case. He said it would be a piece of cake and that he had done all the work—yeah, right! With a lump in my throat and acid accumulation in my intestinal tract, I agreed to at least visit the attorneys in Detroit and let them decide.

An expeditious review of the case file and a quick flight to Detroit and I am in over my head. "But Always Trust Your Cape" (from a song by Guy Clark, check it out). Without dragging this out too long, they accepted me as a sub for Jon, but I had to do an extensive amount of work to complete the work Jon had thought he had done, and to 'fit' the case facts to my approach to testifying. I knew the case was against Ford, but I did not know what monetary damages the plaintiff was requesting. Probably just as well. If I had know what was at stake, I might have been a little, just a little, apprehensive. Instead I just strolled into the lions' den.

Detroit Superior Court—day one—voir dire. This is similar to the Spanish Inquisition! The opposing attorney fires away with a series of question that he hopes will discredit you and any potential testimony. And this he does with a vengeance. Normally the judge will simply rule on your overall qualification and allow you to testify and let the jury determine your worth and the worth of your testimony. But in this case, the judge decided to discuss each of my qualifications that was before the jury and elaborate on each and every one, emphasizing the why's and wherefore's of my qualification. Whoa, score one for the good guys, and me. Either he really liked me or really disliked the defendants attorney. I was elated and my attorney was ecstatic.

At the break, he said, "We got this judge and jury on our side big-time. Now all we have to do is not screw it up."

And screw it up. We didn't. A 12-million dollar verdict! In the 1980s this was unprecedented, especially in Detroit and against a manufacturer. A little elucidation might be in order. It wasn't all me. The main element in our favor was that we had what is known in the trade as a sympathetic victim. The plaintiff was a woman who was pregnant when the accident occurred. When the baby was born it had serious medical defects because of the medication administered as a result of the burns the mother received during the accident.

Secondly, my opinion here, the defendant's attorney was an egotistical, arrogant-so-and-so, and he not only offended the judge as outlined above, but raised the hackles of the jury. I'm sure there was a third strike in there somewhere, or maybe it was just my superb performance. In any event, my 'legal career' was off and running.

A sidebar. That's legal talk for "come over here and whisper in my ear." You really don't want to try an automotive vehicle case in Detroit. Normally the opposing witnesses, including the other dueling experts, are not allowed in the courtroom during the other dude's testimony. But guess what, you can have as many 'spectators' in the galley behind the railing as there is space for. These can include any and all of the engineers from the local engineering facilities. And they can freely pass notes and have conferences during the breaks. So as the plaintiff's 'expert' (me) is opposing an army of the defendant's 'experts.' Actually real experts, although perhaps somewhat biassed. I'm not complaining, just stating the facts, ma'am.

My main source of income during the 80s was from my legal work. As a matter of fact, I got so caught up in the legal biz that I decided to go to law school! What this guy barely made it out of high school. Perhaps a lapse in brain connectivity. I continued to work and went to the local Monterey School of Law. They'd take anybody, I guess. I did OK, not great, but OK.

Then one day I had an epiphany. Here I was making several hundred bucks an hour—yeah, that's right $200 to $275 and hour, circa 1980—doing what I knew, and working to the max. If I became an attorney, I would be starting from scratch and be at the bottom of the barrel. I would also probably have to throttle back on my 'expert' workload while attending school. At this point it seemed like I was not headed in the right direction, so I pull the plug. At least I learned the basics.

As I've said before, at least I think I have, being in the right place at the right time means more than having a rich uncle. Ford Park-to-Reverse cases were in vogue just as I stepped up to the plate. I had set up a test fixture at Jon's shop and soon began to inherit a number of these jewel-like cases. Yes, there was a problem but lawyers, being the hound dogs that they are, were jumping into the brouhaha with all four feet. As a result of this intense activity I began to collect a number of frivolous cases. Yeah they were Fords and yeah they had automatic transmissions, but how about the fact that the driver forgot to put it in Park, or the linkage was in such disrepair that only a weldment would have kept it in Park. You get the picture.

Now, the attorneys were pleasant enough. They would tell me that they just wanted to know the truth. Well, sort of. Only if the 'truth' favored their position in the lawsuit. After a few unfavorable 'truths,' the phone wouldn't ring. In the beginning of any litigation, the manufacturers would dig in their heels and pay nada. So the plaintiffs need a champion in their corner who would say the 'right' thing. But by the mid 80s the pendulum had swung in the other direction, in my opinion, and I thought it was time to pull up stakes and move on down the road.

Even in the good times, it wasn't all peaches and cream. The majority of the work was in L.A. (that's Los Angeles not Louisiana). This required a lot of flying or driving between Monterey and L.A. As I mentioned before, at one point I kept a car at the LA airport, right along the major flight path. An old junker Plymouth Horizon. After a while it was coated with jet fuel, but that only improved its appearance.

The rest of the work was everywhere but home. I traveled the country— first class. I think I was in a courtroom at least twice a year, sometimes for days at a time. Truth be told, I really enjoyed the verbal battle between myself and the attorneys. In the more than ten years that I was active in this arena I only got burnt once and it was my own fault. My attorney would not let me do the testing that I thought was necessary. Regretfully, it came back to bite me.

When I first started, Jon laid out the 'rules.' Don't charge any less than the maximum going rate and always fly first class. Apparently this establishes your worth. Interesting concept, but that's the way of the legal 'profession.' Nough said.

But on the good side, this little detour into the legal profession saved me financially. Without this enhanced income, I would never have been able stay in California or do what I did on the other side of the horizon. Stay tuned there's more to come and you'll see what I mean.

10 I HEAR THE ROAR AGAIN

Sometime around 1984 (no, not that 1984, sorry George O.), I heard from my old friend Bob Tullius. At that time he was running the GTP program for Jaguar throughout the U.S. He was based in Virginia and had a shop to die for. He was preparing to run in the LeMans 24-hour event and they especially needed some help in converting from their Weber carb setup to Fuel Injection. Could I help?

In the past I had done some cylinder flow work and produced a cylinder head for them. There were several other little design projects which may or may not have been integrated into the engine program. I just can't remember the details.

For the LeMans effort, the English Works was footing the bills and they wanted to incorporate a Lucas FI system. They apparently had plans to team up with Lucas for future production packages. Lucas flew in a team of engineers and I went to Virginia to work with them. Things got off to a real bad start when I walked in and started with the Prince of Darkness jokes.

"Why do the English like warm beer?—Because they have Lucas refrigerators." Very few laughs. As a matter of fact there was dead silence. It took Bob a few days to mend the fences and get peace across the pond.

So now to work. The power baseline was to establish with the Webers. The Jaguar V12 used six dual barrel carburettors, three on each bank. This provided a single throat for each cylinder, essentially an IR (individual runner) arrangement. About as good as it gets for max power and the complexities of the Weber carburettor made it quite drivable. The first few runs with the FI were low on power. Based on my work with the various Chrysler FIs, I wasn't surprised. You may recall my earlier preaching, but to ease the burden on your memory I will restate.

The first cut with the FI had the nozzles located down low near the manifold/cylinder head interface. The fuel from the Weber exited high up in throat of the venturi. As I and others have learned, when the fuel enters the air stream high up in the inlet runner it cools the intake charge and makes it much denser, therefore providing a more packed combustion mixture, and ultimately more oomph. It took a bit of convincing (how about a lot) for the Lucas dudes to agree with my proposal. Needless to say, we inched up the trumpet a wee bit at a time. I'm sure we did a little trumpet length survey, can't really remember, but basically we maintained the overall runner length of the Weber setup. We really didn't have the luxury of an array of backup development engines like the ones in my past lives.

After a few days of romancing the stone, we were able to equal the output of the Webers with a little fattening of the torque curve. The big change was in the bsfc (brake specific fuel consumption), in pounds of fuel per horsepower hour. The Weber setup was in the high 0.4s and the FI managed to get into the mid 0.3s. That, my learned reader, is about 25 percent! Now, there's no guarantee that these numbers will carry over directly to the vehicle on the track, but you'll realize some improvement in fuel mileage. Over 24 hours, that could mean at least one less pitstop. In the end this was the winning vote for Tullius. He was discouraged over the lack of power gain. Drivability would probably be the same, although I would vote for the FI, especially under the varying conditions at LeMans. As I said, the potential improvement in fuel economy was the winning card. I'd better be right. And I was!

By the time all the smoke cleared and we were LeMans-bound with the completed FI package, it was 1985. It was huge operation. Shipping the cars, equipment and people-types to France was an enormous undertaking, which thankfully I managed to circumvent. I just showed up in France at my assigned time and place.

One interesting event is worth mentioning (there'll be more). It tested my mettle and once again renewed my faith in the hard-working crew guys who usually get very little credit.

First practice session. Brian Redman first out, couple of laps he was back in. Motor appeared fried. Peanut gallery wisdom stated the mixture was too lean, "change the fuel brain EPROM, and pull the spark back." Wait a minute, who's the engine boss, me or them? A little rollback, please.

During the early stages of the FI development program, I had asked for some sample fuel from France. It turned out to be fairly difficult and probably would not arrive in time to do any testing. I compromised and just asked for the octane specs, which I got and I was satisfied.

Now back to France. I was immediately accused of misjudging the fuel and mapping an incorrect spark curve. Could be, but I doubted that backmarker wisdom. I insisted on cool heads to prevail and requested the cylinder head to be yanked.

While this was being performed, one of the crew guys came up to me and began to whisper in my ear. I always have time to listen to the crew guys; they live with this stuff 24/7. My guy asked whether we had purged the fuel lines.

What you say?? At LeMans the fuel is supplied by the track and is fed into the pits via an integral piping system. Who knows what fuel was in the system from the last event or how long it had been in the system? Any team of worth immediately drains several barrels of fuel and dumps those into their transporters. Now the system is purged and ready for the race cars.

Whoa, big daddy, I guess the burden is back on me. Okay, drain the cars, purge the system, leave the cars alone and let's do some laps. This decision did not go unopposed but I had Tullius's vote, so it carried the day. The mystery was solved and the cars where humming like Jaguar V12s hummmmm.

Race day. Glad to report the engines ran fine, for a while. Car 40 DNF, lap 151, broken halfshaft, Jim Adams, Brian Redman and Hurley Haywood. Car 44, finished 13th, Bob Tullius, Chip Robinson and Claude Ballot-Lena, but not without a bit of drama.

It was sometime in the early morning when the 44 car came into the pits with a disturbing beat provided by a no longer functioning valve. Immediate inspection placed the culprit in the rear cylinder right bank. Brian Krem, engine builder extraordinaire, and I surveyed the situation and deemed it a catastrophe, but our 'never say die' sensibilities deemed otherwise.

The tech heads and our fearless leader, Bob Tullius, got our grey matter together and formulated a plan. We decided to 'fix' the valve, wait until just before the 24th hour tick, generate a single lap and be declared a finisher. LeMans rules require you to cross the finish line after the 24 hour mark in order to be declared an official finisher. Good plan, but how do we 'fix' the valve? Brian, Lanky Foushee, and I devised a plan that seemed beyond comprehension but doable, we hoped.

As follows: Brian grabbed the biggest and heaviest hammer in the tool box and began swinging it with full vigor at the camshaft just before the last cylinder. We all crowded around in hopes that no paparazzi would make a permanent record of our minor transgression. Success: the camshaft had parted and the valve no longer functioned as intended. Lanky then came up with the superbly brilliant idea of lifting the remaining bent valves and filling the port with spray insulation foam. Great Stuff as advertised. The piston was a little beat up but it moved up and down with minimal trauma.

And then we waited. The clocks seem to be retarded and it took forever to reach our launch time. Finally drive time approached and Bob eased out the clutch and was gone off into the fray.

Ah, but what a tangled web you weave once you practice to deceive. Old 44 ran much better than we thought and Bob went past the finish line before the appointed hour 24, which meant we had to complete at least one more lap. The finish of the race was a complete madhouse with fans storming onto the track from everywhere. The hordes were so massive that the officials stopped all but the first few finishers down at the last turn. Bummer. We knew we couldn't idle down there for long.

But at last the racing Gods shined upon us and the remainder of the competitors. It turned out that parc ferme was right there where they had stopped the remaining cars, so wisdom prevailed and the remaining finishers were hustled directly into the corral and our day was done and our butts preserved. Thirteenth, not good, but it could have been worst except for some quick and free-thinking lads from across the pond.

Au revoir Français.

11
REST THE BRAIN, WORK THE BODY

<u>Time-Shift</u>—*Now. Some of you may wonder why I injected this 'Life' into a book that's primarily automotive. Good question. Hang on, I'm a little out of my element here trying to vent philosophical. But I believe it's simple—its all about the competition. It's all about moving at ten-tenths. It's all about pushing the limit and getting back just in the nick of time. Some may call it adrenaline, some call it passion, some call it obsession, but whatever the common factor is, it's hard to ignore. If you haven't experienced it, I don't think I could get you there. It filled a very necessary gap in my life which I hadn't realized I needed.*

IN 1986 MY WIFE LIZ convinced me to take our first vacation. After all, we had been married for 28 years. I guess it was time. Place of choice was Hawaii, the Big Island. Just by chance we ended up in Kona. I didn't have a clue, darts on the board. As predicted, by me, I was antsy after a few days. I wandered into a sports shop and picked up a triathlon magazine. What? Are these guys crazy? Swimming, biking and running without stopping? No way.

But wait a minute this could be a serious challenge. You think, no, but maybe? I must confess I had a bit of a head start that I should mention. In about 1975, during my spare time, I commandeered my son Bobby's bicycle and started touring around the Coast Highway. One day I was motoring down, so to speak, PCH and a couple of biking dudes passed me by. For whatever reason, I decided to latch onto their little train. After a few miles they signaled they were slowing down and waved me over.

They asked me if I had ever raced before. I said no—at least, not bicycles.

They said, "We tried to drop you as best we could and were not able to. You're pretty fast, you should try racing."

And so I did.

Okay, now ten years later and 2500 miles away—Hawaii. While I was in the sport shop I decided to buy a pair of running shoes. I figured I had some background in biking and I had spent a lot of time in the water, swimming, surfing and scuba diving. Now all I had to do was put one foot in front of the other and move on down the road.

I laced up the shoes and went out for a little run. Weather report—100 degrees, 90 percent humidity. One mile and I was history. I had to walk back to the motel, defeated.

But for some reason I couldn't let it go. I continued to run, farther and faster. Back home on the mainland, after a few months I decided to enter a triathlon in Bakersfield, California. It was hot and then it was hotter. The swim was in a shallow lake, could almost touch bottom as you stroked, the bike leg was hilly but uneventful for me.

But one thing that stands out in my mind is the swim-to-bike transition, i.e., changing from wetsuit to biking clothes. Neophyte that I was I ran to my bike, carefully removed my wetsuit, toweled off and slowly put on my socks and biking shoes and biking helmet. Mounted my steed and was off down the road. Now, for anyone with triathlon sense this was a colossal waste of time. Races can be won or lost in the 'pits,' i.e., the transition. This changeover took me minutes instead of seconds. I had a lot to learn.

A note for those who might care: This is how it should be done. Just like auto racing, your time in the pits (transition) can make you or break you.

Most triathlon races require the use of a one-piece wetsuit, so I'll start there. When you return to shore, as soon as you can stand and begin running, grab your zipper lanyard and unzip the suit and then pull down the top to your waist. When you reach your bike completely remove the suit and drop it.

There are numerous ways of mounting your bike. I found the following to be most advantageous. Before the event begins I clip my bike shoes into the pedals. I then take a large rubber band (not too stout) and secure the far side pedal (right side for me) to the frame seat post in the up position. The left pedal, of course, is in the down position. My bike helmet is loosely placed on the handlebar. My first task is to put the helmet on and fasten the chin strap. If I need it, I put on my singlet and/or competition number. I then quickly place my left (bare) foot onto the top of my already mounted left shoe. I mount the bike and immediately begin pedaling with both feet. Both bare feet are now located on the top of their respective shoes/pedals.

After I cleared the transition area, I insert one foot at a time into its shoe while continuing to pedal. I have Velcro straps so they are easy to cinch up. Meanwhile, I am still pedaling in start/stop fashion until both feet are secure. On the return to the transition and before coming to a stop I remove both of my feet from their shoes and place them on top of the shoes so I can keep pedaling, hard if I have to. As soon as it is safe, or I think I can get away with it, I loosen my helmet strap. The bike is then dropped next to my wetsuit as well the helmet.

Preparation for the run is minimal. I use the same singlet as on the bike. Running shoes are key. I used a slipper-type shoe that required no lacing. But I can run in anything. If you need a supported shoe, consider using lace locks that will secure the laces without having to tie them. No socks, they waste time. If it's a hot, sunny day you may need a light cap. That's it—you're now headed for the finish line.

Because my biking performance was good, even considered very good by some, I was often asked what my 'secret' was. The short answer is—none. My approach to competitive biking was to never stop pedaling! I mean that literally. Never coast—on the flats or downhill. You need to select the proper gearing so that you are always hard on the pedals, even on the downhills, especially on the downhills. I think you get the idea.

The race—back to Bakersfield. After my shameful transition I completed the bike leg in a reasonable time frame. But the run was a burden all its own. I lumbered my way out of the bike area and started to 'run.' At best it was a walk but more of a gimpy hobble. My legs just did not want to work. I talked to them, but to little avail. I stopped and turned around a number of times, but then convinced and conned myself to return and continue. On more than one occasion I received encouraging words from a fellow sufferer.

Finally I was at a point where it was probably just as arduous to return as to continue. So I endured. After much consternation and inner conversations I finished, sort of. There were about 675 entrants and I finished 673rd. Just ahead of two old ladies who were carrying on a conversation as they crossed the finish line.

My son Bobby was at the finish line. He smiled and asked where I had been. He said he was about to send out the paramedics to fetch me. He thought I was face down in the dirt.

But all was well in my pea brain. I loved this sport and was determined to persevere. And persevere I did. The following year I won my age group at this same race and went on to be a terror of the 50-ish age group. For several years running I was ranked in the top five, and in actuality I was number three in the country. There were only two guys who could beat me, but unfortunately we met on several occasions. One of such occasion was THE Ironman in Kona Hawaii—full circle!

Unfortunately—there is always an 'unfortunately' attached to my tales—I got so engrossed and consumed by the competition and winning, of course, that I trained and raced every chance I got. The view at the top is somewhat distorted for those looking up. To continue to be as competitive as I was, I needed to train twice a day, every day, morning, noon and night. Not much different from cars and motorcycles, as we'll forthwith see.

Many folks often wonder, and some ask: Why, am I, or others, so good at what we do? Here's my take. **You do well at what you do because it's what you do well! Got that?** If I start to pursue an activity, whatever the setting, and do it well, I continue. If I'm continually shitty at it, I drop it. Simple survival. Heart surgery, anyone? More to the point, you will never see me on a golf course, I suck. OTOH, part of that might be because I have no desire to chase a little ball around with no real excitement involved. Some might call it talent, or lack there-of. But to each his own, no offense intended.

MAIN EVENT KONA—HAWAII

1987 IRONMAN, KONA, HAWAII. It's a bit ironic as to how I got there. To participate in the Hawaii Ironman you have to qualify in a sponsored event. Bakersfield, California was such an event. It was the race where I won my class and qualified for the Ironman. But remembering back, this was the event where I finished nearly dead last less than two years earlier. Now, that's some serious effort, and a few good genes. More about that later.

The Hawaii Ironman is a major, major event. Parties, parades, lots of food (gotta stock up) and a bit of last-minute training. Actually the training is mostly a matter of acclimating to the temperature and humidity in Hawaii: 100 degrees F, 90 percent humidity.

You can live a clean life but you never know when disaster will strike. I was out for a ride on the bike when I heard a crack and, oh shit, the seat-post broke. I had to ride standing up for about ten miles to get back to the condo. Just a touch of apprehension; some might call it panic. Off to the bike shop only to find there were no seatposts that would fit my bike. I might mention that my seatpost was a lightweight aluminum post with trimmed sections (you just can't help it, once a racer always a racer). The best I could do was to get a steel post from Honolulu the next day, less than ten hours before race start. Next day, a quick pit stop and I was ready and relieved.

The Kona Bay. Hundreds of bodies floating around and jostling for a spot. There's no qualifying here just everybody for himself. The usual pre-race adrenaline pump and the only way around that is to put on your race face with the one thousand yard stare and visualize the events in their entirety.

Bang, off we go. At this point you've got to be extra careful not to get whacked with a series of elbows in the face. Next, you look around for someone who's just a tad faster than you and latch onto them, be it a him or her. The tow is impressive, not unlike Daytona, just a few miles per hour slower.

The swim is 2-1/2 miles long, the water temperature is mid-80s and that's hot! We swim out and around an anchored boat and back to the pier where our two-wheeled steeds are silently waiting.

Now, I must confess I am not a fast swimmer. I'm a strong and tough swimmer, just not fast. A swim coach once suggested that my kick was so bad I should give up kicking and save energy. Thanks Coach. I was 22nd out of the water. About 55 guys in the 50-55-year-old class, not good. When Liz announced my position as 22nd I was totally deflated. She reported this position placement as I was on the bike climbing a steep hill to get out of the pier transition area. I almost fell off the bike. It hit me like a heavy body blow. But a quick shake of the head and game face back on. After all, biking was my major forte.

Focus, focus. Each age group was designated by a letter. I think ours was H, carefully branded on our calf with a Magic Marker. Focus, focus Chasing Mr. H, chasing Mr. H was my mantra, 112 miles out and back.

I didn't carry a water bottle, mainly because of the extra weight, and also because I have trouble absorbing water when I'm physically flat out. By the way, the attire for the day was bike shoes, Speedo and a helmet. No shirt and no sunscreen. We don't need no stinkin' sunscreen.

Every 15 or 20 miles there was a water station. Mind you, I was one of the hard-core. I didn't stop, just slowed a bit. I would grab a bottle of water pour it all over myself and toss the bottle. Can't carry that extra weight, you see. Next, we had the choice of various fruits and, bless the gods on high, chocolate chip cookies. I'd grab a bag of those heavenly morsels and literally stuff them into my mouth in one big handful. Crumbs everywhere, but the sugar rush was awesome. Back down on the bars and hard on the pedals. I forgot to mention that the standard biking position is head down and elbows on the special tri-bars. Aerodynamically efficient. I'm here to tell you it all counts. You would only sit up at the water stations.

I was nipping off the competitors like leaves in a hurricane. The bike leg finished on the far side of the town and then we would run back through town and onto the main course of the marathon. Lava to the left and lava to the right; it truly did look like a moonscape, 26.2 miles of beautiful Hawaiian landscape, just for our enjoyment!

I was pretty sure I was in third or fourth place by the end of the bike leg. I believe I set an age group record at five hours and 20 minutes, averaging 21 mph for the 112-mile, very hilly course. But we were very fortunate that year: the winds were mild, never at our backs, but mild.

I got off the bike and I could barely stand up. For sure, I could not stand erect. My back wanted to stay bent. I slipped on my running shoes. And I mean that literally, they were extremely lightweight slipper-type running 'shoes' with no laces. It took me three or four miles to straighten my back and get up to running speed, such as it was.

As I ran through town, my daughter Kristine shouted, "You're in second place, you're in second place, he's just ahead."

Apparently I had passed 21 competitors during the bike leg. I was stoked, but at this point a cautious pace was paramount. I could see the leader, but could not close the gap.

We turned around at the halfway mark and headed back to town. But at about the 16-mile mark, I was beginning to shuffle just a bit slower. Then much to my horror I was passed. No way, I said, but I could not respond. Lactic acid had had its way with my lower extremities.

To make the last few miles pass more quickly for you than they did for me, let me just say that I finished in a discrediting fifth place. Fifth out of 55 or so competitors, or as we say in professional racing, fourth loser. I planned on setting a new age group record and winning my age group. Nothing less ever crossed my mind. I did set a new course record—10 hours and 32 minutes—but so didn't four other guys. It was an awesome field. Of the top five, two of us were from the U.S. and the other three were from Europe. A truly international field.

It took me several years to recover financially. When you don't answer the phone, they move on. Emotionally I'm not sure I ever recovered. Such is life in the fast lane.

I continued to race and continued to win, but eventually my day job became more demanding and more financially necessary. On to another life.

But wait, wait, I promised I'd talk about Jean, Gene, no genes. Many people dream of having a crystal ball that could predict their future. Well, I discovered one, but it was the essence of the double-edged sword. Let me 'splain.

Through my extensive reading about human physical performance, I discovered the term VO2 max. Google states:

VO2 max or maximal oxygen uptake is one factor that can determine an athlete's capacity to perform sustained exercise and is linked to aerobic endurance. It is generally considered the best indicator of cardio-respiratory endurance and aerobic fitness.

But in addition to this intriguing definition, I further discovered that the National Masters Association and the World Association of Veteran Athletes had accumulated reams of data correlating VO2 max and human performance, and related it to age groups. After reviewing the data, I concluded, rightly so, that once you determined your VO2 max you can predict your endurance capabilities, i.e., running and biking, at any distance. So being a true man of science, I decided to test the theory on yours truly.

Cut to the chase: I was evaluated, my VO2 max was determined, and I set off on a journey to prove the validity of these reams of data that existed. IT WORKED. I cross-referenced my VO2 max for running distances from one mile to a full marathon. And I'll be dipped in cottage cheese—it was spot on, every time. I had the crystal ball that could predict my future.

But wait, I soon realized that it not only predicted my abilities, but, shit fire, it also exposed my limitations. Once you got there, there was nowhere else to go. It was flat discouraging to come face-to-face with your real limitations.

Then I began to consider other gene potentials/limitations and, as you might guess, there were limitless combinations. If it's a fact that our physical potentials are controlled by our genes, then so can our mental potentials.

I have no answer, but I truly believe that this is a truism. Someone much smarter than me once said, "Be careful what you wish for, you just might get it—and find that you really don't want it."

Well, I have more than exhausted my philosophical and prophetic capabilities so I will let you, the reader, get what you can from this esoteric BS and move on down the road. It is what it is.

12 BANGLADESH—SAVING THE WORLD—PARTE UNO

Not all was lost in this last diversion. The phone did ring and I did make a few call phone calls myself.

Sooner rather than later, I got a call from an old friend and one of my crew lads from the Javelin race car program, John Hutnick. He had gone on and graduated from grease monkey and welder to become a pretty crafty car designer. He worked for Alain Clenet on his Clenet Cabriolet car project in Santa Barbara, California.

Anyway, he contacted me about a new project he was working on in Goleta, California, a neighbor of Santa Barbara. He had designed a jitney vehicle for eventual manufacture and distribution in Bangladesh. Whoa, that's different. This would turn out to be one of a number of save-the-world projects that have and will cross my desk. That's a good thing, but most, if not all, have turned to dust. It is what it is.

I mentioned that John Hutnick was a car designer. I think I need to clarify designer and designer. There is the artsy-crafty designer, styling studio type. We'll refer to him as an industrial designer. And then there is the engineering, nuts and bolts type of designer. John was the former and I am, on the other hand, of the latter persuasion. So be it. We need each other although we are constantly bickering over form versus function. A debate for another time.

John had formed a design group in Goleta headed up by Bill Jennings, and they were in league with an entrepreneurial group from Bangladesh to design and build a prototype bus-like vehicle for eventual manufacture and sale in Bangladesh. It had to be of simple construction because both materials and labor in that country where minimal. Having local manufacturing capabilities was a controlling factor in this project. The bus was meant to replace those god-awful motorized tricycles/rickshaws. John had already completed the design of the bus, made molds and was in the process of producing their first prototype fiberglass body. Their problem was that their chassis and powertrain designer was way behind and apparently very, very lost. Old Turk to the rescue.

John and Bill assured me that it would be a minimal task, just look over the existing chassis and powertrain design drawings and, with a few strokes from my magic pencil, all would be well. Not so, optimistic, but not so. Voltaire once pronounced that, "Optimism is the madness of insisting that all is well when we are miserable," and truly in the shit (addendum by me).

I was soon to learn a tough lesson of being a consultant—long distance relationships just do not work. After a few back and forth efforts, I had to pack up and move down to Goleta for what I thought would be a few weeks, but ended up being a little over a year, the first of a number of these long distance relationships.

The design criteria for this project were extremely interesting and a tad bit bizarre. It always rains in Bangladesh, make that, it deluges in Bangladesh. In anticipation of this given, the interior of the bus was designed with a drain in the floor. In conjunction with this, there were no doors or windows. Easy come, easy go.

Also, there was a requirement for easy access and egress on all four corners, because ... there were no maximum capacities on these babies. If you could hoist yourself up and elbow a space, you had a ride. A vehicle that would logically carry perhaps eight to ten passengers would be motoring down the road, such as they were, with twenty or more bodies hanging on and carrying on with their neighbors while casually talking, smoking and eating. As I said, bizarre, but there you have it—the essence of mass transportation.

Fortunately we had access to a number of talented craftsmen who were willing to work under extreme pressure. As I completed the chassis design, the frame was formed. As I completed the suspension design the components were eased into place. The powertrain, engine and transmission took a little more effort because the working parameters kept changing. Top speed, acceleration rates, and hill climbing capabilities were all a constantly-moving target. The engine type and size was also subject to change, weekly. Finally everything came together in a magical moment—the money guys were in the air and on their way to sunny California. A deciding factor, as it were.

We managed to build a running prototype. Drove it around town, up and down hills and over dales (what the hell is a dale anyway?), perfecto. The money dudes from Bangtown showed up to participate in the festivities with smiles from ear to ear, handshakes and smiles all around. The prototype was loaded onto a plane and vanished over the horizon, never to be seen or heard of again.

I mentioned saving the world. This wasn't exactly a volunteer no-pay job, but the intent was to do good. Make work for the people of the country, switch their thinking from two strokes to four strokes, and make a little profit for all involved. An electric version was discussed but wasn't practical. But greed set in early in the program. Back at the source in Bangladesh, brothers, cousins and nephews all wanted a piece of the non-existing pie before it was cooked or even made. Not to worry, I got paid. Most of the costs for the program were covered, but that's not what it's all about.

Accomplishment, pride in seeing what you have created and put to its intended use. That's the real reward. Of course, the money doesn't hurt. If you slip and fall, just get back up and face the abyss head-on. Just be aware that it's looking back at you. Edison summarized it so eloquently: "I have not failed. I've just found 10,000 ways that won't work." I was starting to realize this once I cut loose from the race biz and its focus on winning at all costs.

What's next?

13

LET'S GO TO INDY!

I MISSED MY CHANCE to get into Formula One when the Shadow/Don Nichols operation failed. Was this a second chance? We'll see, my friends, we'll see.

A few years before this tale begins Keith Black had been contacted by Jim Feuling—that's spelled Feuling but pronounced 'Fueling,' got it? Jim had been working on a Quad Four program for the Oldsmobile division of GM. He had been quite successful pumping up the output of that little four cylinder. He and his cohorts had designed a replacement aluminum block and wanted KB to cast it and then machine it. Because of all that KB and I had gone through, and learned, with the Chrysler 426 Hemi aluminum block, he wanted me to look over the design and pronounce it fit for consumption.

I drove down to Ventura, California, where Jim's shop was located and met with him and his design crew, namely John Bristow. I was truly surprised at the excellent quality of the detail drawings, very impressive. It took several hours to walk though the drawings but basically I felt that they had done an adequate job with the design and I only made a few suggestions regarding the casting details.

The machining was straight forward. A very limited number of the blocks were produced, primarily for a closed course speed record attempt with A.J. Foyt at the wheel. That year, 1987, the Oldsmobile Aerotech vehicle, with the Feuling Quad Four, set the close course record at Fort Stockton, Texas, at 257.123 mph. The vehicle was most definitely a GM Tech Center production but, although I have no real proof of this, my feeling was that much of the nitty-gritty aspects of the Quad Four engine design, if not all, slipped through the cracks at the Tech Center and made their way to the West Coast.

Jim and I stayed in touch over the years. In some ways we were alike, but in other ways we were total opposites, go figure, but egos can do that to you. Jim was a true gear head. He lived and breathed cars, primarily engines. He was a masterful promoter, primarily of himself, which is good—somebody needs to do it. He was also a patent junkie. He had over 100 patents to his name. Valid? Who knows? In my opinion the US Patent Office needs some serious attention.

Somewhere around 1994 Jim was at an IndyCar race and was introduced to John Menard Jr., owner of an IndyCar team that was using their own version of the Buick V6. Apparently—I wasn't there—Jim was orating about his capabilities in the realm of engines and in particular, his accomplishments in the area of aluminum. The outcome was that they set up a meeting at Menard's shop in Indianapolis, or somewhere back there where those guys are comfy. Jim immediately got on the horn to his 'old buddy' Bob Turk Tarozzi—that's me. "How would you like to go to Indy?"

Uh, let me think about it. Thirteen seconds later I was packing my bags and heading south.

Jim and I flew to Indy to meet with John and the rest of the team. Then the fun began, the shit hit the fan and landed I know not where.

The knights gathered forthwith at the table round. It really was a round table, although I think I was the only knight errant. Jim Feuling, John Menard Jr., and his right hand man, Larry Curry, and I were gathered around. The following scene could have been scripted for As the World Turns or some such soap opera. John introduces Jim and me and puts forth the proposal that we would design and build an aluminum block to replace their existing cast iron version of the Buick V6. The silence was deafening to the point you could have heard a feather drop.

Larry Curry slyly stated, "Well, John, I too have just initiated the design of an aluminum replacement block with Dart Industries of Canada. I was just about to inform you."

Yeah right. John Jrunior swallowed hard and, in an effort to save face, he hesitantly proposed that they undertake both projects, and may the best man win.

Total bullshit! What followed is beyond comprehension. Mr. Menard (I need to distance myself) further proposed, primarily to Jim, that because of my immense expertise in the area of fine designed aluminum I should forthwith travel to Canada to critique the Dart design. A total cluster f**k is developing at the speed of light.

I called a recess and conferred with Jim. "What the hell are you thinking, other than nothing?"

Jim states that this is a clever ploy wherein we will have the inside track to the Dart design and therefore be able to better them and beat them to the goalpost.

Believe me, I couldn't even begin to make this shit up. I protested, but to no avail. I should have pulled out right then and there but the draw of Indy glory was too strong and therefore I acquiesced. It was all downhill from there.

I traveled to the Dart facilities in Canada, on my own without even returning to California. The Dart program was more than 'just initiated;' it was well under way. They had six designers and engineers on the program. I just took in the scene and nodded my head. I'm sure everybody was convinced that this was a major fiasco in the development stages, and it truly was. I returned to Ventura, the check had arrived so the double-pronged mishap was underway.

This was not an easy transition. I needed to be in Ventura at the Feuling facilities—full time. Oh shit, another move. Somehow I persuaded my wife Liz to sail with me on this voyage, unlike my previous move to Goleta for the Bangladesh extravaganza. The clouds where aligned. My daughter Kristine was free and available so she took on the task of managing our domicile in Carmel Valley, along with our dog Buddy. Pack it up and move on out. We rented an apartment in Ventura and settled in for what was to be a year-plus adventure. Better stated, a misadventure.

This was to be a monumental undertaking and I needed to prop up the engineering staff, such as it was. Jim's shop and shop personnel where adequate, but the design staff was lacking. First cut, you call on your friends. First I recruited Allan Junor, the son of a close friend of mine. Next I ended up with a quasi-celebrity in the name of Preston Hagman, son of Larry (Dallas) Hagman. Larry was a close riding buddy (Harleys, of course) of Jim's. Initially I thought this would be a burden, but it worked out well. Preston was well versed in the design software area, which we were about to need desperately. I added a few other designers, including the ever capable John Bristow of Quad Four fame.

Equipped with this eclectic workforce, I charged ahead full steam. One of the most necessary aspects of an undertaking like this was to bring together a cooperative effort between the chassis/car guys and engine guys. Essentially this meant that I needed maximum cooperation from the Menard shop personnel, especially Larry Curry. Not going to happen. I was stonewalled at every turn from day one, make that minus day one. This operation was the essence of 'off to a bad start.' I needed chassis drawings in order to determine the engine attachment points. This was especially important because the engine was a stress member of the chassis.

First I got the familiar "they're in the mail," then, "England is making changes," then "a new chassis is due soon," etc. I was attempting to expedite matters by telephonic communications.

Then one day I got a memo from Larry Curry, and I quote, "Any items that you would need in the future for your projects I expect to receive a written request form. This request should be directed to my attention (sic) only then you will receive a response back in writing. The telephone calls are becoming disrupted to all of the many projects we have going on here. Thank you."

Well, there you go—the beginning of the end. I made a few additional attempts to mend the bridges, but without success. Finally I was compelled, by my alter ego, some may say evil ego or self destructive ego, to take pen to paper with my version of a poison pen letter. I craftily summarized the events to-date and concluded with the following:

"... I have gotten the distinct impression that their (read Larry Curry) attitude is that we (Feuling guys) can do what we want as long as we don't bother them, I find this attitude unacceptable."

The End. The money was pulled and communications ended. By the way, I did copy Jim with this correspondence and he was in agreement. I sadly began to fold my tent and pack my pencils for the long drive home.

But wait—'It ain't over till it's over!' Jim had one last request of me. Apparently he had been negotiating with Harley Davidson for quite some time to provide them with a West Coast development source. And again the clouds were aligned. The new HD Chief Engineer was Earl Werner, who had just come over from the Corvette division of GM. Earl had known of Jim from the Oldsmobile Quad Four program and was himself very performance-oriented. They wanted a sit-down meeting in Milwaukee and Jim wanted me there as his 'engineering staff,' ace in the hole or asshole, whichever you prefer. So off I went.

14 CHANGE HARLEY, SAY WHAT??

THE MEETING WAS SMALL but the ideas were intense. Jim was there primarily to promote his three valve cylinder head adaption of the Harley Dee. Earl liked the idea but saw problems with the 'not invented here' syndrome. I don't remember who first proposed the idea, but we were soon discussing the concept of making a one piece crankshaft for the Harley. Earl's general thrust appeared to center on bringing Harley into the 20th century, HD's reluctance to change notwithstanding.

To those of you not familiar with the HD crankshaft design, it consists of three pieces which have to be pressed together at assembly. This was done primarily to accommodate a one-piece connecting rod, usually with a roller-bearing assembly. Truly an antiquated design.

The rest of the world was using a one-piece crankshaft with a take-apart connecting rod and a Babbitt bearing. Not exactly rocket science, but it was foreign to HD. The one-piece crankshaft would allow higher engine speed, better component life and should be cheaper to manufacture and assemble. Because of the fact that the HD cylinder banks were in line, i.e. not offset, the connecting rod assembly was a fork-and-blade arrangement, somewhat complex.

In order to eliminate this complexity, I proposed a master and slave rod arrangement. Hey, it wasn't my original idea. They were first used on the WWII 18 cylinder Pratt & Whitney airplane engines. Is there anything really new? Hold on, let's relieve the seriousness of this tome for a moment.

Master and slave rod. I used these terms because it was part of the nomenclature of the original design work. As soon as my first drawings hit the HD folks, I was immediately taken to task—what again?—for the politically incorrect term of 'slave.' I was instructed to revise the drawings and other paperwork to reflect a more PC-acceptable term. After many man-hours of contemplation I choose the eloquent phrasing of 'master and link assembly,' smoothing the paths of cooperation.

Onward and upward. I won't bore you with all the details of the design process. Suffice it to say that everything went reasonably well. All the components were modeled in CAD using solid modeling techniques. During the earlier Menard project, we were fortunate to have the assistance of Preston Hagman to help us sort through the software quagmire. Contrary to popular opinion, it is very difficult to interchange CAD models and drawings between the various software packages. Believe me, I've tried on various occasions and it never—I repeat, never—worked without extreme difficulties and drama.

Once you have the components modeled, it's a piece of cake to generate the various orthographical projections required for adequate dimensioning of the castings, forgings and machining. All you have to do is get inside the component part and become one with the mechanism, sort of Zen-like, I kid you not. I can't speak for all designers, but my way is the way to a successful design: become one with the machine.

Let's take the crankshaft for an example. Perhaps I would position myself on top of the piston looking down the connecting rod (conn rod for short). I would observe the loads coming at me from above and from below me. I could also see the movement of the crank along its length, flexing as it rotates. I might even be able to feel the vibrations as the speed changes. Okay, you think I'm nuts, which I won't argue with, but I'm here to tell you it's the way I do it and I believe it works. At least I have a decent track record.

Speaking of vibrations, here's a tale that could only be true because it is. A little levity, please.

One of my design parameter studies for designing a crankshaft is a complex analysis of the cyclic balance loads. I had done this on numerous occasions, starting with the various stroker crankshafts that I designed for KB. Generally speaking, the balance percentage falls somewhere between 52 and 54 percent of the piston and rod weight. The present twin cylinder design was just a little different, so I decided to ask the crankshaft gurus at Harley what percentage balance weight they were using on their current production crankshafts.

After several phone calls with resulting silences at the other end of the line, they stated that they would get back with me. Okay, fair enough, this could be top secret stuff. Finally I got a call back from the head of the engine design group who stated in substance that they really didn't know why they were using the value that they were using. It was apparently part of the Harley Davidson history (mystique), but it was about 66 percent. Well, I'll be damned, maybe, about, ask Willie G, who the hell knows.

As I stated before, I couldn't make this shit up, nobody would believe it. I felt that the only logical way of establishing an acceptable balance percentage was to build several engines with various balance weights, insert them into test bikes and turn them loose on HD's tried-and-true engineering elite.

And so we did. Three motorcycles where built up and fitted with conventional three-piece crank-shafted Harley's at 50 percent, 54 percent and 66 percent balance configurations. In came the Harley troops complete with their favorite riding gear. It was a very interesting day, to say the least. The bikes where driven by everyone in attendance and the selections were blind and at random.

Bottom line: they couldn't tell the difference! Oh, they noticed that the mirror shake was a little more pronounce on bike A, no, maybe it was bike B, and so it went until the sun set slowly over the Pacific Ocean on another fruitful day.

Because of what I determined to be more favorable bearing loads, I elected to build the one-piece crank test engine with 54 percent balance configuration. The rest of the story was uneventful. I ran two engines on the dyno primarily for baseline durability. Just a few hours. I left the hard core, hours-upon-hours, for the Harley dudes back in Milwaukee. I packed up the engines and associated spare parts off to the hinterland and waited for the verdict. And waited and waited. Alas, it never came. My job was completed, and in a very timely fashion I might add, but decisions from OEM folks are hard to come by. At least they did run the engines and pursued the design concept. They changed the configuration of the link rod for easier machining and revised the oiling scheme a few times, but in the final analysis it was parked and I have never seen nor heard of a Harley Davidson three-piece crankshaft. Some folks just cannot accept change, the process of becoming different, and that describes Harley to a tee.

Time to get home and feed the dog.

15

WHAT ANOTHER HEMI FUEL MOTOR? YOU GOT TO BE KIDDING!

IT STARTED BEFORE I even left for Ventura. For many years, Brad Anderson had been trying to get me to design a Hemi fuel motor for BAE (Brad Anderson Enterprises). I had turned him down on each occasion because I didn't want to just duplicate the existing KB block, and, quite frankly, I was devoid of fresh ideas. Then one day I had an epiphany, a vision, lets just call it a new idea.

The original KB aluminum block was designed with water jackets. Early in its life the use of water was eliminated, but the jackets remained. At this point the 'water jacket' was used primarily for weight reduction. There was a drawback in that there was a lack of support material behind the liner. My 'brilliant' idea was to fill the void created by the water jacket and in turn provide substantial support for the liner.

Why I, or anybody else, hadn't thought of this before belongs in the category of not seeing the forest for the trees, or the trees for the forest, whatever. Obvious, right? There was also the consideration of providing streetable engines wherein they would need water cooling. This brings the designer to the dilemma of making a product that fits all useable categories but is not really useful for anyone. Think on that for a while.

Now, if I just filled in the water jacket void, the block would gain a substantial amount of weight which is an unforgivable sin in this business. However, by carefully removing weight, from the exterior of the block and then reinforcing the thin sections with ribs we produce an intriguing-looking and lightweight block. Best of both worlds, function and form.

La-di-da.

It took a while, but once the design was modeled and before we started making the patterns and core boxes, we started to shop for a foundry. This procedure is a very significant part of the whole process of manufacturing a product, especially a casting. You don't just show up at the foundry one day with your completed tooling (core boxes). The foundry and any manufacturing process, for that matter, has its own specific requirements for handling and implementing the tooling to make a finished product in their facilities. I usually contact and involve the foundry as soon as possible, <u>sometimes even during the</u> design process. No sense designing something that can't be made. Same thing when it comes to selling the product. You can't sell a widget that nobody wants. I'm sure you can get an argument from a super salesman-type but you won't convince me.

The search for a foundry was an arduous one. As I had mentioned before, a very important part of the casting process is to be able to heat-treat the finished casting within a very narrow window of time. We finally located such a foundry that also had their very own metallurgist on staff. Will wonders never cease? Brad and I tripped on over to said foundry and sat down for a chat. After a tour of the facilities I presented my foremost requirement: we need to achieve 42,000 psi in selected sections. The immediate response was, "No way, never happen."

Once again I had to prove my point. Words were not enough. I gathered a sample of one of the existing KB castings and had them do a few tensile pulls to validate the strength of the material. Once we had determined the validity of my words, of wisdom I proceeded to explain how we could get there from here, and they proceeded to listen.

All seemed well in the foundry biz and the casting began to flow, no pun intended or maybe there was? However, as I explained before, the foundry is a terrible place to work and it is not conducive to producing consistently good work. Soon the voids began to appear and castings were rejected at an ever-increasing rate. Some flaws were not discovered until the machining process began. At this point, swords would be drawn and a battle would begin as to who would foot the bill for the rejects. Not a pleasant sight.

Brad was clearly getting discouraged and was considering pulling the plug on the whole operation. NHRA to the rescue. Suddenly NHRA decided that the cast blocks could no longer be used for Funny Car and Dragster application. Forged blocks were the order of the day. There was already a forged block in use and perhaps a little politicking was in place. Forgings are stronger, but at about 375 to 400F all the alloys approach the same yield strength. The improvement is really the toughness of the forging, its resistance to impact. Means a lot when you throw a conn rod or crankshaft piece at the side of the block with very high values of momentum. Ouch.

It's interesting how NHRA always talks about keeping the cost down when new designs appear, but throws caution to the wind when it comes to TV time. Think about it. When a failure occurs and the track is oiled down, TV time is affected and so are the purse strings. Safety is the spin but money is the speaker. Better move on.

Brad said that he had to dump the cast blocks and switch to forged blocks or get out of the block business. I told him it would not be a problem. The solid model of the block that I had developed could be forwarded to the forging plant and be massaged with their specific forging tooling software. Interestingly, most of the blocks today are forged at the same facilities. They make the tooling, specific to your design; they own the tooling, produce the forging and also maintain the tooling. You pay a fee as well as the cost of the forging. Somehow they manage to juggle this to everyone's satisfaction.

The forging process is minimal with regard to shaping the block. They start with a cube of aluminum. The sides or 'Y' shape of the block is forged. The valley chamber is forged in with straight sides. The crankshaft area is similarly forged with straight sides. The ends are left un-forged to allow more freedom in machining. The complete block is between 85 and 90 percent machined. That's a lot of chips.

So Brad moved into the arena of forged blocks and I just moved on, again.

16

BACK TO VENTURA AND HARLEY D.

ONE DAY I GOT A semi panic call from my buddy Jim Feuling, that's spelled Feuling but spoken as 'Fueling.' Harley Davidson had a new project they wanted to feed to Jim and he would like my presence in Ventura to help him evaluate the technical aspects of the proposal. Just a simple one day, in and out. It's a long drive for a one day meeting but what the hey, I'm off again. The Brad Anderson job was just about completed and I needed something to fill the void.

The Harley chaps were in attendance in force. The leader of the gang was one of their chief engineers, Bob Kobylarz. BK had an interesting way of conducting a meeting, especially when it was a lengthy presentation such as today's offering. We were all gathered in the conference room with the table in the center, rectangular this time not of the round variety. Bob would write each point of the presentation on a two-foot by three foot-piece of newsprint and then attach it to the wall with tape. He would continue this method of presentation until all four walls were completely covered with sheets of newsprint and then he would start a second row. We would be completely engulfed in paperwork, as it were. It made for an interesting hour or so, questions to come later.

Oh, I forgot to mention what the presentation was presenting: Eric Beull and AMA racing with the Harley 984 air-cooled twin. It was interesting enough to keep me in my seat.

As you may know, Eric Beull was an ex-Harley employee who struck out on his own to produce the Eric Beull line of motorcycles. He had an inside track to the works and was able to procure purebred HD engines, no clones. He had several hiccups in his ventures. First hiccup HD loaned him money to stay afloat, then somewhere along the line HD purchased the company but left Eric in the driver's seat. I think that's where we were at this point in time.

Eric had been lobbying with AMA (American Motorcycle Association, not American Medical Association) to allow him to run a 1000cc air-cooled engine against the more prevalent 600cc water-cooled mainly Japanese engines. He then pitched HD to get on board and develop a special racing version of their 984cc air-cooled engine. He would produce a special racing chassis to pop the engine into. Unfortunately, this didn't happen until many years later, but that is another story and not part of my purview. Onward and forward and back to our paper-encircled meeting of the minds.

The meeting was coming to a close when, lo and behold, there on one of the presentation sheets appears the name 'Bob Tarozzi—Project Engineer.' "What the f**k,, hold on just uno momento. I am here to consult and advise but I ain't, I repeat, I ain't riding herd over this here monstrosity." I stand to emphasize my point but I stop short of walking out, contrary to my more usual romp. I will regret this later, but let's take it one stride at a time.

Meanwhile, Bob K makes the point that without yours truly the program will not be offered to Feuling R&D. After all, without me there is no real engineer at Feuling R&D. He further states that he wants me on board because I am **'an engineer's engineer.'** I must admit, I got a little weak in the knees, just short of tears. I think I am beginning to cave.

Jim calls a pause in the proceedings and asked me to take a stroll to his office for a momentary sidebar. In the confines of his office Jim tells me that he really needs this work and without it, he is likely to go down the proverbial tubes.

I stated, "I am not coming down here again, rent an apartment and go through the trauma of moving again."

Jim counters, "You don't have to rent anything. I have an apartment in a hangar at the Santa Paula airport where all my motorcycle collection is stored. You can stay there. It's a huge apartment and is fully equipped."

"I don't have an extra set of wheels and I am surely not buying anything for this type of venture. Santa Paula is twenty or so miles from here."

"Not to worry, I have a number of vehicles floating around the shop that you can use any time. And I'll cover the expenses for your trips back north, anytime."

I still didn't like the idea of moving down to Ventura for another potential fiasco venture. But I am weakening. Then comes the coup de grass.

"Listen, I'll throw in a $50,000 bonus at the end of the program, and that should be less than a year." Jim was pushing.

What could I say? In retrospect a lot, but I caved and agreed to head up the program. Bad clouds were forming but I failed to open my eyes. OTOH, perhaps my eyes were open but I failed to see.

Back in the meeting, the HD folks were overjoyed and more newsprint was pitched at the wall. We all agreed that a meeting with Eric Beull and his design staff was in order. And off we went to Wisconsin.

There were meetings galore, lunches and handshakes all around. I came away with one major conclusion—this wasn't going to work. Beull and Feuling were so ego-driven that the tension between them could not even be pierced with a chainsaw. Bob Kobylarz agreed to assign a liaison engineer (referee) to keep the peace. He had had dealings with Beull in the past. Long-short, it didn't work, the liaison was useless and problems developed almost immediately.

I was designing the engine package which consisted of new cylinder barrels and fin package. A new cylinder head, incorporating the Feuling patented three-valve arrangement and a complete Fuel Injection system. This would also include the exhaust system which is where clashes popped up. Beull's design staff was well underway in their task of designing the frame. It took a month or so to get them to agree to send me a CAD model of their frame design. By the time it arrived, I was also well along on the engine configuration, including the exhaust system. Guess what, they both wanted to occupy the same space. Somebody's got to give up some real estate. At first I was adamant about not yielding, Jim more so. Finally I was willing to change the exhaust configuration if necessary, but Jim would not move.

To be fair, it was more than just the exhaust piping, it was the location of the exhaust port. It would have required some serious gymnastics. With neither party willing to move, we proceeded to build the engine as designed and leave the match-up until a later date. As I stated above, the egos were immense and totally destructive.

We elected to use a prototype casting method for the cylinder heads and barrels. The prototype foundry would accept our CAD model of the head and produce a core without the interim step of tooling, i.e., molds. This was a relatively new process and would produce a one-time-only set of cores in very rapid order. The cylinder barrels were also made by this procedure, as well as the FI system. It was a prototype nightmare, but it went along quite smoothly with just a few bumps along the way.

Dyno time. The engine was bolted up to the Superflow engine dyno by our steadfast shop magician, Allon McBee. I had earlier been committed to predict, or perhaps better, propose, an output bogey. After grinding out the numbers and checking the direction of the wind currents, I advised that we could make 125 bhp on the dyno. Roll on.

Before the HD/Beull engine was bolted up to the Superflow, we had evaluated several production Japanese 600cc bikes on the DynoJet chassis dyno. The best of the lot was the Suzuki GSXR 600cc bike at 90bhp at the rear wheel. Neither Feuling nor Harley ever ran any direct comparisons between chassis and engine dynos to determine a valid powertrain correction factor. I stood out on the limb and proposed six percent. No objections? There you have it, a number. The corrected output of the Suzuki would then be equivalent to 95.7bhp at the crankshaft. So my proposed 125bhp at the crank was more than adequate, if we could get there from here.

Back to work. Considering the complexity of the engine and fuel injection package we were elated when the engine breathed fire after a few spit-backs. After the run-in we began the power runs with intermittent leak rate checks.

We reached a 'grand total' of 112 bhp at the crank, which would equate to 105 bhp at the rear wheel. This was at 8000 rpm. Needed a lot of work on the valve train. For some reason, because of cylinder head combustion chamber size or perhaps the piston configuration we were limited to 11:1 CR. I was proposing 12.5:1.

<u>Time–Shift</u>—*Today it would be at least 13.5 to 14:1. The years gotta learn you something.*

But don't scoff at those power numbers you doubting Thomases or whatever your name is today. This is a first cut and we haven't even looked inside the little darling. But, alas, on the last leak check the numbers were off the chart, so off she (it) came and onto the bench.

The autopsy was nail-biting and glum. As soon as the heads where removed the problem was evident. The valve seats were no longer in their assigned stalls; they had escaped the clutches of their aluminum surroundings.

A little explain. The heads were produced by a fairly new process and with a company I had never dealt with before. After the valve seat failure, I did some checking—yeah, after the horse gets out, close the barn door. I know, I know. In any event the foundry shipped the castings to us devoid of any heat-treating process. Now, if you have been reading along diligently, you will remember how critical the heat-treating process is to the final strength of a casting. Well, now you can see the results of neglecting that step in the operation—disaster. But what the hey, that's part of cutting-edge technology that tests the soul. Onward.

"Okay Jim, I'll just regroup and engage a tooling source I know and make a regular set of core boxes for the cylinder head and the cylinder barrels as well, and we'll be up and running in no time. We still have to settle the exhaust system and chassis collision situation," says dumb, stupid, make that naïve, me.

Jim calmly states, "Oh, by the way, we're out of money, the budget is exhausted. We have to work with what we have."

I'm totally blown away. No more money, impossible, absolutely impossible. Because the checks didn't come directly to me, I let the Feuling accounting gal handle that end of the program. I had my hands full with the direct design work and directing two or three designers and engineers to do what we did.

Then, after I came back down to earth, I had a re-think. We had an initial budget north of one mil and we had been working for six to seven months. It just didn't make sense. But I had it up over my eyebrows. The clashes between Jim and Eric were always present and made my life very difficult. I put on my 'f**k you guys' hat and demanded additional funding to complete the task as originally proposed or I'm outta here. I'd done it before and I can do it again.

No response from either Jim Feuling or the powers to be at HD, so as Jackie Gleason so elegantly put it, 'and away we go.'

I believe the engine pieces and drawings were sent back to HD. They elected not to continue the program. One other major factor was that Eric Beull was never able to sell the AMA on letting him run the 1000cc HD air-cooled engine against the 600cc water-cooled engines currently in the series. As I stated before, a number of years later he was there and did well. The three-valve Feuling cylinder head was never a consideration. One, because it need additional work, but more significantly, it 'was not invented here.' Egos trump.

<u>Time–Shift</u>—I attended Jim's funeral sometime late in 2002. Jim had passed away from pancreatic cancer. There were many friends and business associates who attended. One of the guests was none other than the Harley Davidson VP of Engineering, Earl Werner. I had dealt directly with Earl in the past and I felt comfortable enough to talk to him about the Feuling/Beull debacle of years past. I explained to Earl that I wanted to apologize for the failure, at least my part, of the Beull engine program. I indicated that I had no idea, not even a clue, that we had consumed the entire budget in such a short time.

He said, "Not to worry, Bob. Jim and I were shifting monies from the Beull engine program to support the W3 engine design and development program. We were planning on incorporating the W3 engine into the HD lineup. Unfortunately Harley turned us down and all was for nought."

Politics in the fast lane!

Ironically, I did do some work on the W3 engine program in between my other duties. Unaware, of course, that I was shooting myself in my very own foot. To enlighten the readers, the W3 engine was a morphed Harley Dee Twin Cam, with a third cylinder grafted onto the crankcase to represent a W configuration. My part was primarily to design and produce the conn rod. The W3 conn rod was similar to the one-piece crankshaft conn rod except that it had two lugs attached to the master rod and two connecting links. Worked like a charm. Little did I know Peter was in there robbing me to pay Paul.

Let's move on.

17 A LITTLE DIVERSION

For all you hard-core gear heads, you might want to skip this next section. I am going to reveal my competitive side again in the arena of running, i.e. placing one foot in front of the other. After all, it is part of another Life.

Before I had agreed to move on down to Ventura to shepherd the Feuling/HD project, I was well into the Northern California Pacific Association running series. This series consisted of ten races ranging from a one mile effort to a full marathon. At the time I was dragged down to Ventura, I was in the lead for the championship and was leading by 50 points. Not bad for this old man.

BTW, it was an age group event so I was leading my age category, not the whole schlemiel. Ventura is just north of Los Angeles, which is essentially Southern California. The race events were all in Northern California, so I had a distance handicap to overcome.

I devised a dubious plan to continue my participation. I would fly from Santa Barbara, a stone's throw from Ventura, to San Jose, on the southern end of Northern California. Liz, my devoted wife, agreed to meet me in San Jose and then drive us to the race event, sometimes several additional hours north. We usually stayed in a motel overnight, attend the race event, and then she would drop me off back at the airport after the event. I would be back at my station on Monday morning. And it worked. I maintained my lead, although I was not able to place numero uno every time.

The weeks passed and we were nearing the end of the season, just two events left, and I was still leading by those precious 50 points. But fate stepped in and reared its ugly head. My back spasms were close to debilitating. I carefully scrutinized the last two races, one half marathon and one full marathon. I could, and had, struggled though shorter races with a bum back, but a half and full marathon, essentially back-to-back, was just not fake-able. I decided that with my 50 point lead I could afford to miss the last two races.

Bad decision. As it turned out, the marathon was worth double points so when the last checker flag dropped, I lost by two points! Again first loser. I was devastated, so much so that I could not attend the awards banquet. Now, some would call me a sore loser and they might be correct, but until you've walked, nay run, in another mans moccasins do not—I reiterate, do not—criticize. End of story, this one anyway.

And life went on.

18 ENGINE CORPORATION OF AMERICA—SAVING THE WORLD— PARTE DUE

FOLLOWING THE FEULING/BEULL disaster I was back in Carmel Valley, waiting for the phone to ring. True to form, AT&T reverberated in its familiar tone. On the other end was an old Chrysler/KB buddy, Bob Mullen. He was down in Southern Cal, more specifically Fullerton, involved in a new engine project. To wit, a monster single cylinder, opposed piston, engine/generator package destined for Third World countries expressly to light up entire villages. So as stated above, once again, a save-the-world project.

Bob wanted to know if I would be interested in developing a set of working drawings of the engine. He indicated that they had a series of layouts and now needed detail drawings. By nature I despise the chore of trudging through detail drawings. In the past I even hired detail munchkins to perform the task and relieve me of that drudgery. However, when the coffers are below sea level you tend to do what you didn't do when you did what you did. I took the job.

The company was named Engine Corporation of America (ECA) and located in the depths of Orange County. I motored on down to meet with the boss man, Dr. Marius Paul. He was originally from Romania and had a very interesting history. He was plucked out of Romania by our very own CIA. He was then deposited somewhere in Texas and put to work in one of our, the USA's, top secret high altitude aircraft programs or some such cloak and dagger activity.

Once he completed his obligation to the Feds he was cut loose to do his thing. He decided to utilize his rocket science and thermodynamics background and apply them to ground vehicles. He hooked up with DARPA

(Defense Advanced Research Projects Agency) and convinced them that he could apply the thermodynamic Brayton cycle to achieve a high output, high efficiency tank engine. They bought it and he was in business.

A little insight into the Brayton cycle; even I needed some help on this one.

From some geek-like website: *The Brayton cycle is a type of thermodynamic cycle typically used to depict the way <u>gas turbine</u> engines, <u>jet aircraft</u> engines, and other turbine engines work. The Brayton cycle can be used in both <u>internal combustion</u> engines as well as <u>external combustion</u> engines. The original Brayton cycle engine consisted of three basic components: a <u>gas compressor</u>, a <u>mixing chamber</u>, and an <u>expander</u>. Today, the Brayton cycle is used almost exclusively in gas turbine engines, which typically consist of a gas compressor, a burner, and an expansion turbine. The two primary uses of gas turbine engines are electrical power generation and jet aircraft propulsion.*

You can see where I'm going here, or maybe not. In any event, Dr. Paul was determined to apply his high altitude turbine knowledge to an internal combustion, two stroke engine like we drive around in every day, sort of.

The good doctor was claiming several hundred horsepower from a 1.5 liter engine on any fuel. But here's the kicker: It would perform this task under the efficiency umbrella of 90 percent and spew just liquid water out of the tailpipe.

"Holy impossibility, Batman." But they did it, well, almost. In order to approach this colossal feat they had to make some compromises (cheat?). There were no existing turbochargers that could achieve the pressures required. So they pumped high pressure, high volume air into the engine from portable air compressor units.

But woe unto those who spin a tangled web. There was nary a fuel injection unit that could inject fuel directly into the cylinder at these extremely high pressures. The first distillation was to decrease the intake pressure. Then they could successfully inject the requisite fuel load, with conventional FI, due to the lower intake pressure. The engine ran and produced a reasonable level of power at about 45 percent efficiency, only a touch better than a conventional combustion ignition engine (read diesel). The discrepancy in efficiency could be theoretically accounted for by the absence of the turbos. Turbos use the exhaust energy to spin their wheels and develop intake pressure, thereby increasing the overall efficiency of the engine. I hope you got that. If not, stay tuned.

What did Edison say about 10,000 failures? Dr. Paul had 9,999 to go. I was about to participate in number two. All of the above exploits occurred just prior to the first sand war, a.k.a. Operation Desert Storm, a.k.a. Save GHW Bush's Investments. Word came down to Dr. Paul that he would have to cease development work on his baby because the Federal monies were needed to produce real tank engines for the upcoming activities over in the sandbox. So with brakes full on and his head swimming in knowledge, he had no forward motion.

Fortunately the Feds allowed Dr. Paul to continue his work in the private sector as long as he did not tread on classified info. Everybody was apparently happy and Dr. P. was going to create an even bigger version of what couldn't be successfully run before. If you get my drift.

Let's review. We will start with 3000 cc (183 cubic inches) and develop scads of horsepower. Dr. Paul was a little loose with his HP numbers. I think at one point he was going on about the equivalent of four Cadillac engines. But suffice it to say it would be capable of running a multitude of kilowatt electrical generators. Fuel requirements were essentially non-existent. It could run on any fuel, liquid or gaseous, including panther piss. With the high pressure turbos in the mix, the overall efficiencies would be over 90 percent.

The coup de grass, in my estimation, was the free water out the tailpipe! For every pound of fuel you burn, you get a pound plus of water. If you don't believe me do the chemical reaction analysis. You remember your chemistry, don't you?

In your everyday vehicle you don't see this outpouring because the hot exhaust gases evaporate the water. Except at startup on cold mornings. Oh yeah, I see said the blind man. You remember the turbos I mentioned?

To generate the extremely high intake pressure required, the Brayton cycle extracts virtually all the energy from the exhaust and the predicted exhaust temperature is well below 200F. Now you get it—no more water vapor, just aqua. Not yet drinkable but with a little more chemical action—viola! Potable water for the masses.

Enough science; I can tell you're starting to doze. Let's get on with the main program.

ECA had been into its commercial application of the Dr. P's engine for about a year when I was contacted by Bob Mullen. Sorry for all the cross talk. We can now get down to business. When I arrived at the ECA works, Dr. P immediately gave me his pitch on the engine's potential capabilities. I will admit that I was a wee bit skeptical but Marius Paul was a convincing preacher. In any event, I was there primarily to produce some drawings. I didn't necessarily need to be a believer. That would come later.

DMP (Dr. Marius Paul) gave me a set of his layouts, which were schematics, of sorts, not even close. I instantly dubbed his layout 'cartoons,' They were funny but not hilarious. The layouts contained numerous cross-sections. The problem is well documented in Drawing 101. None of the areas of the cross-sections were defined, none, nada. I could not tell what was steel, aluminum, air, water or oil. They were all included somewhere on the paper, but they lacked details. It's all in the details, believe me.

`Back at my office, the first thing I did was to color each area in an effort to define the cross-section of choice. Then I went back down to Fullerton to meet with DMP. Once that was sorted out, I went back to my office and began to create.

Over the years I have found that developing a CAD solid model was necessary to my thought process. I could think, visualize and create much better when everything was in 3D. Of course, 3D is a misleading term because the actual CAD model is developed and viewed on a flat screen, but it is envisioned as a three dimensional object. Got that? So my first task was to translate DMP's cartoons into a 3D CAD solid model and then, like magic, the orthographical projections, 2D detailed drawings, fall into place.

With these results in hand I once again motored to the south. You will note that there was no mention or thought of moving again! When the good doctor saw the CAD solid models, he went ballistic with joy. He came out of his chair and gave me a gigantic bear hug.

"You are my angel. I need you to work for me and model the whole engine."

How do you respond to a statement like that? I just said, "Okay lets get started." Plus I had to get loose of his bear hug; he was of generous proportions.

And started I did. I went back to my office and began what turned out to be the longest and most intense design project I ever undertook. I was locked onto and into the computer screen for six days a week, ten hours a day, month after month. At first I didn't even notice the time or duration. As I've explained before, I would become one with the process. I was walking though the water jacket and strolling past the oil galleys, visions of crankshafts and pistons dancing in my head. 'Twas the night before casting time—enough, back to reality.

I contacted a pattern shop that I knew could handle a project of this size. And speaking of size, I had earlier indicated that this was a monster. Let me elaborate just a bit. The bore was 120 mm (4.7 inches) and the stroke was 130 mm (5.2 inches), with two opposing pistons, a total displacement of 3000 cc (183 cubic inches). That in itself was not too overwhelming. But due to the high pressures anticipated and the cooling requirements, the overall dimensions were every large, to say the least. The 'block' itself was over three feet long. But when I added the crankcases, crankshafts and gear drive cases at either end it was as long as a pickup bed, full size.

Oh, and did I forget to mention that each piston had two connecting rods dangling from each oil-cooled piston, and they in turn grabbed hold of twin crankshafts? One set of twins at each end. Rube Goldberg would have been proud. Additional bulk would be appended to our mammoth motor by adding two or four generators onto each of the four crankshafts, depending on how many light bulbs you had. And so it went. Somewhere in the photo section I have included a few photos of our creation. Check them out.

Everything came together with less trauma then I had expected. Time was a primary ingredient. The machining process produced a few hitches, but they were overcome. The entire engine was assembled and rotated by hand—well, with several hands, shoulders, etc. And then we found ourselves at an unwanted intermission. Similar to the smaller tank engine, we were planning to supply shop air to the engine during the initial running because we—make that I—was still in the design stages of creating the monster turbochargers, complete with water jackets to cool the expected high temperatures. But this time Dr. Paul was determined to provide adequate fuel pressure for the injection process. He was off in the Land of Oz somewhere and the FI was not quite ready for prime time. Meanwhile, disaster stuck our little community and the Feds moved in!

Amazingly as it might seem, this entire project was being funded by a single gentlemen. Both he and Dr. Paul where philanthropists of the highest order. I told you this engine was destined for Third World countries to light up their universe. The money man had invented a very useful medical device which I knew little about and had more money than God. He felt compelled to do good and so he was funding this 'light the world' project.

However, he apparently had a lot of free time on his hands and was immersed in other projects to make his already massive pile even larger, which is okay if you play by the rules. BUT he apparently didn't, or so sayeth the SEC, the dreaded and all-knowing United States Securities and Exchange Commission. They felt he did something they didn't like. I think it had something to do with building pyramids, not unlike the Egyptians, but different? Anyway the bottom line was that they seized our main man's assets, which included his bank accounts, which included all his do-good projects such as ECA and their 'light the world' dream.

The good doctor tried to develop other funding sources, but the physics and thermodynamic principals were so difficult to comprehend that few were interested. That, along with his insistence on maintaining control over every aspect of the ultimate production, yielded turndown after turndown. We were out of business. An incredible waste.

BTW I had become a believer. I felt his output estimates were a tad high as were his efficiencies. But we could have come close and it was most definitely worth the effort. At least double the existing efficiencies and water running out of the tailpipe! The world would be nipping at our heels. But alas, it was not to be.

I returned to my now dreary office, and I think I too shut down. I never did return to full time design work. I tried, but I think they were all half-assed efforts. I attempted to hook up with a few race teams, Indy and NASCAR, but none would have me. As a matter of fact, I never even got a response from the dozen or so letters I sent.

I was now 65 or so, old but with lots of experience and credentials. Age was probably a factor in the no responses. But I think the fact that I had worked for myself, a self-employed consultant, you see, for so many years meant no one wanted to take a chance. I just closed the throttle and went to idle.

19 HANG ON, ONE MORE LIFE— MOTORCYCLES

MOST PEOPLE THINK, AND I have been told more than once, "You're too damn old to be on a motorcycle, especially a Japanese crotch rocket." Hey, I think by now you realize that I do what I want when I want, sometimes to my downfall. Just remember, "One of the great pleasures in life is doing what people say you cannot do!" Rebel, but with cause.

I gave this move a lot of thought and changed my mind several times, but ultimately decided that I did not want another basket case to assemble, build and constantly maintain. I just wanted to ride! Back when I was 17 or so I indeed bought a basket bike, literally. It was actually in a box, but everything was in a disassembled state. It was a 1950 500cc single cylinder Matchless. I successfully got it together and rode the bugger for almost a year, with numerous breakdowns and repairs.

I had several other machines during those early years, both smaller and bigger, but always better. Then marriage and college, not to mention work, put a cramp in that early part of my life. So, was I about to get a second chance? Yes, I was!

My first steed was a 2001 949cc Honda. Truly marvelous, with 125bhp at the rear wheel and a featherweight at 412 pounds, wet. Getting back in the saddle after all these years was a bit trying. I didn't have any shunts, but I kept dropping the damn thing, usually forgetting to get my foot down in time. Finally I overcame this obstacle and I got up and rode like I was born to be on this strange craft.

What struck me the most was the constant thought that this was were I was supposed to be all along. That perhaps I had squandered my life prior to this juncture in time. Bullshit, of course, but the feeling was always there. Just an old mind losing its grip.

Then one day I got the urge to once again be at the track. I said it was where I was supposed to be. Could it be a second coming? I was about to find out. Off I went. I did limit myself to what is referred to as a 'trackdays.' I felt that to compete at a competition level was achievable, but much too costly. My earning capacity was now very limited and I was just coasting in the financial arena.

Besides, trackdays were extremely competitive, as I would soon find out. The trackday activities were broken up into A, B and C categories, group A being the fastest group. I started in group C and quickly progressed to group A. Now, mind you, there are no age groupings. Within each group you start with young and progress to old, that's me. I had a few offs. No damage to the person but a few repairs required to the machine, some quite extensive. But I was not to be deterred.

I also developed a longing for the open road. I loaded the bike with travel gear and took off for distances afar on many occasions. I always opted for the back roads. On my many trips to L.A., I never once chose the freeways. Once, I got the urge to explore what was left of Route 66. With maps in hand and a GPS on the bars, I traveled the historic route from California to New Mexico. At that point I turned back toward home via Utah and Nevada, again using only back roads. It was an adventure I will never forget. It still brings a feeling of emptiness as I write these words of remembrance. But as everyone knows, and as I am forced to concede, nothing goes on forever. Not even life itself.

Back to the track. After several of these road trips, I had accumulated in excess of 60,000 miles on the Honda. It was time for a new ride. The bike that every manufacturer seemed to emulate was the Suzuki GXSR. How could I not move up to the best of the best? I purchased a low mileage, used 2006 GSXR 1000. It produced 160bhp at the rear wheel and was still only 420 pounds light. And the braking was even more phenomenal. Two fingers on the brake lever was all that was required, and gently at that. Think about it. In order to get this kind of performance in a car, it would cost you several hundred thousand dollars. The Japanese crotch rockets were all under $12,000, new. It's a no-brainer.

Again, back to the track. I was getting faster and loving every minute of it. Even though these were not sanctioned races the competition was intense. Gentlemanly intensement, but nevertheless, intense.

Now, I didn't set any track records but I was sniffing at the tailpipes of much younger lads, and damn proud of it. I was attending trackdays several times a month, sometimes two and three days in a row. On some occasions, make that many, the temperatures were over 100F. On quite a few occasions the younger lads would be packing up at about 3 o'clock. Me, I was committed to get in every lap available until the 5 o'clock bell rang. Obsessed, addicted, you might say so. What else is new?

WHAT AND WHY

OVER THE YEARS I gave a lot of thought to my abilities and limitations. Why wasn't I better, faster and quicker? Good question. I had a lot of experience and I was never frightened or nervous on the track. I was always relaxed. It was my life, this speed thing. Some refer to it as focused. In my opinion that fully describes it. But why couldn't I get faster than the other guys? What were my limitations and why?

Eventually I gathered the following thoughts. It's all about the processing of information! For instance, when you are traveling at speed you have a series of decisions to make. As you approach a curve or turn, you must first decide whether the road goes to the left or the right. Next, you must assess the magnitude of the curve and how fast it can be negotiated. In many cases you must also evaluate the road condition and adjust the speed bogy as required. Overshadowing these parameters is the regulation of the vehicle itself. Gear choice and related engine speed. How and when to apply the throttle. There are other judgments that need to be made, but these are the essentials.

The time required to assimilate this information is what separates them from us. This applies to young lads versus time challenged gentlemen such as myself. You can extrapolate this to cover the elite car and motorcycle driver/rider. This is what separates the men from the boys, but in this instance, it acts in a negative manner. As one ages the ability to process data diminishes and one slows down. I'm applying this to man and his motor vehicle, but if you think beyond, it also applies to life itself. An albatross of sorts, which can be extremely difficult, more likely impossible, to disregard. Well there you have it. My esoteric and uninformed take on concepts that are over my head. However, I leave you to cogitate on their meaning and truth.

Youth is wasted on the young!

ALL GOOD THINGS COMES TO AN END

FINALLY I HAD TO FACE reality. As you get faster the toll on tires escalate, to the point where I would use up a set of tires at each event. At $300 a set, it was getting costly. The bike itself was trouble-free and required very little maintenance. But you had travel: gas, motel bills and food. I traveled all over the state, anywhere there was a track available. Addicted, you bet. But when the addict and his family, run low on cash, changes must occur.

On top of all that, my family—wife Liz, son Bobby, and daughter Kristine—insisted that I act my age. I strongly disagreed, but I won't admit to how old I was at that time; however I think you can figure it out. So I sold my trusty stallion along with all its accoutrements. A sad, sad day. This was one of the hardest decisions of my life. It was the first time that I had to 'voluntarily' quit and move on. But that is what I did. Unfortunately I had nothing to move on to.

EPILOGUE

A NUMBER OF YEARS have passed and I am back at idle, waiting for my next Life to tempt me into action. There were various other ventures and schemes that I was involved with over the years, none worthy of lengthy mention. They brought in a few shekels but most, if not all, turned to dust. That is the life and times of an independent consultant. But when that phone does ring the spirit soars.

To fill a particularly dry period, I decided to venture into the dusty realm of furniture design and construction. True to my basic temperament I immediately began to accumulate the 'necessary' tools to the point where my two car garage could no longer shelter my vehicles. I had to design the pieces because that's who and what I am. I found this activity very pleasant and rewarding for an old codger.

As with my automotive design processes, I found it necessary to follow the design stage with the actual doing stage. My hands no longer got dirty, they got dusty. I must say that I created some very exquisite pieces. One particularly outstanding piece was a rocking chair fashioned after the very famous Sam Maloof rocker. If I had to guess, or estimate, I would say that my rocker could sell for between $8,000 to $10,000 dollars. But it contains too much of me to let it go. I have included some of these pieces in the photo section.

Of course, I can't forget the writing of this book, which was a very daunting task. In the beginning it was slow going because writing was 'foreign' to me. Lest you forget, I was a high school English dropout. Who knew? I hope you will be merciful in your judgment of my current dissertation.

It all started in a very casual manner. I got a call. There's that phone ringing again, always a good sign. Anyway, I got a call from Cliff Gromer, editor of Mopar Action magazine, for an interview. He was sicced onto me by Dr. Bob Reed of Bakersfield, California. I had been interviewed a number of times during my tenure in the automotive biz, but this was to have a very different outcome. Cliff spent over six hours taping my endless verbalizing. Once I get started, I'm hard to shut off. Sort of like a dieseling engine.

Cliff went back to his office, transcribed the recordings into neat little bug-book packets. He then emailed them back to me for approval. When I read them I didn't recognize myself. Who was this guy talking back at me? Cliff's prose was perfect, but that ain't me. I revised the text to conform to my unorthodox speech pattern and suspect command of, or perhaps lack of respect for, the English language, and returned it post haste.

The clouds were aligned and Cliff ran with it. Same agenda for part two and part three. At this point Cliff suggested that I just write the articles from the git-go and he would publish them under my byline. And so it went. As they say in the book biz, I had found my voice.

Several months went by after the last article was finished and I had a flash of insight. I would assemble these words of wisdom from the articles and put them together for my kids and grandkids. So they could see what that guy was about. My kids, Bobby and Kristine, lived through all that happened, but I don't think that they really understood what I did and, more importantly, why I did what I did. My grandkids, Sage and Bodhi, of course wouldn't have a clue. They were not there.

Some might call what I proposed a legacy. Too pompous for me. I prefer—just a little insight into who and why I was what I was. Takes more words, but I like it better.

From this point it just grew into an ever-increasing and ever more complicated task that I just could not avoid doing. The doing turned into a full blown published book for all to see and read. For real? I started slowly and with difficulty, but then the words just started to flow and they seemed to make sense. Of course I'll let you be the judge of that.

And for those friends of mine who have encouraged me to write this tome, I sincerely thank you one and all. I hope you enjoy what you started.

There were other lives sandwiched in between those I've thus far so scrupulously recorded. Some of these cost me money as opposed to bringing in the cash, a negative cash flow as such. I thought I would include them here, lest I forget them myself.

For a few years I worked on occasion with my good friend Paul Rossi. At that time he had a very successful race team running in the IMSA sport car series. At its peak, Paul ran five Chrysler Talon race cars, two with paid drivers, the remainder rent-a-racers. We also ran a group of cars at Pikes Peak. But that's really his story, not mine.

Because of my interest in data acquisition, I accumulated my own data acq equipment and landed a few gigs. Most notable to me, few saw the finished commercial, was a production with Chrysler and hot shoe Emerson Fittipaldi. A few other non-productive attempts and the equipment went onto the shelf to gather dust along with a few spider webs.

Then there were a couple of seafaring non sequitur adventures that were very serious for me in their relative time and space. I needed to clear my head from the failing times I was facing. I took the time and effort to learn, with diligence, the art of sailing. I quickly worked my way up to a 40 foot ketch, singled-handed. I occasionally 'let' Lizzy 'help' me. We bare-boated these babies, i.e. rented them on location for a week or two. We covered the Florida Keys, numerous Caribbean Islands and the San Francisco Bay—not for the faint of heart. But here I was again abandoning my telephone that was ringing into an empty office. Time to reverse direction and get back to work. Ugh. By this stage in my life, I think I was losing it.

Along with my sailing fascination, I developed a deep interest in scuba diving. The logic—you got a boat with water all around, in most cases very warm water. Why not jump in and have a look-see. If you've followed my ventures so far, and read between the lines, you good and well know I'm not a halfway person. So off to scuba school I went and got certified as a PADA scuba dive instructor. Dove all the wrecks I could find in Florida and the Caribbean. Came back home and instructed and toured folks throughout the gorgeous Monterey Bay here in Central California. A wee bit chilly after the warm and scenic waters of the Gulf. But this Life, as with sailing, was encroaching on my office time and ultimately my bank account. You see were this is heading. Yet another ending of a Life dictated by work. Not the adventurous 'work' of that former time and place where I was able to pursue … ah, it's over, how sad. It is what it is.

∞ ∞ ∞

I WOULD LIKE TO take the time to thank those who saw in me something I myself will never understand. They were mostly bosses of sorts, but not in the traditional sense, who somehow pushed me ahead of them to swim and survive on my own. They pointed me in the direction they wanted me to go and then left me on my own. Most of all, they listened. I'll never understand the whys and wherefores of what they saw, but I am truly eternally grateful for their faith in me.

Ed Petraeus at Worthington Pump, Tom Hoover, Pete Hutchinson, Larry Rathgeb at Chrysler, Keith Black at KBRE and Brad Anderson at BAE. Thank you, one and all.

There you have it, my friends—an unrestricted account from a time gone by and not to return. Thoughts of time running away, fleeing into the cosmos. I miss them one and all, but it is what it is.

I would welcome any comments or questions you have about anything contained herein. I'll answer to the best of my ability and I'll try to keep it short, if that's possible. I can be reached at rtarozzi@yahoo.com. I look forward to hearing from you all. And if you have the time and can muster the inclination visit my website www.rtarozzi.com

Thanks for reading and remember those immortal words:

> Life's journey is not to
> arrive at the grave safely
> in a well-preserved body,
> but rather to skid in sideways,
> totally worn out, shouting
> "Holy Shit ... What a Ride"

Sincerely,
  Robert 'Bob' 'Turk' 'Squeak' 'BobO' 'Fast-Bob' Tarozzi

∞ ∞ ∞

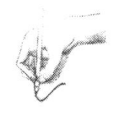

Part Four

Tarozzi Photo Album

Words are great, photographs are greater. They're recordings that are unaffected by the frailties of the memory. Words tell the story, photographs reveal the details, life as it was.

I didn't have the time, or more to the point didn't take the time, to document all of the events that took place in my Lives. Fortunately friends, and sometime strangers, have been thoughtful enough to pass on to me some of our mutual histories captured on film. I will be forever grateful to these folks.

On occasions people have asked me if, at the time, some of the projects I was involved in would stand the test of time and still be around to this day. Hell no! At that stage they were just jobs, just a segment of time. I do not want to belittle those jobs and projects. Do not misinterpret the term 'just jobs.' It's mainly that I was forever looking forward to the next project, or perhaps I should say looking upwards. I was motoring down the road at 100+ miles per hour and had to keep my eyes on the road. I cherished those jobs!

There is currently a youthful mantra stating 'live in the moment.' Sounds good, but I never had the luxury, my mind and my soul would never allow it. I had to keep moving and as my tales have told, and these photographs will depict, I did just that.

I have carefully sorted these recorded memories in a chronological order that follows the text; which I'm sure you have carefully read and committed to memory. And so—to the images of my Lives.

The Early Years — 1955 to 1965

The Automotive Years — 1965 to 1980

The After Years — 1980 to 2013

Enjoy!

The Early Years - 1955 to 1965

Our gang, preceding that faithful day. My Dad's in the center surrounded by Strokers of questionable character. This was truly a time to preserve.

My True Love. My Wife, Sweetheart, Lover, Parent, Friend and Buddy. I'll love you always.

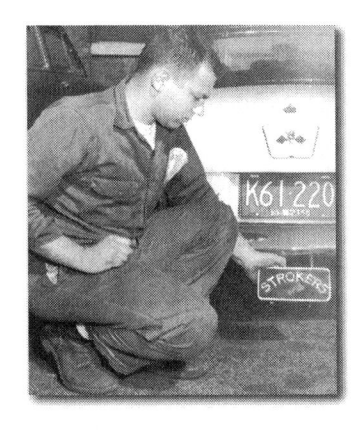

The first and true Turk. Proud a few pounds but proud of what and who he was.

The Holy Trinity. Tom, Ed, and the Turk. Overshadowing their creation. The '32 roadster with borrowed Chevy.

'32 roadster up close. Not much to look at, but oh so quick. The professional lettering set it off from the ordinary.

One of several blown Healey/Chevys to hit the streets and strips. That's a 671 peeking though the hood.

At the wheel. One of my few rides in this hell-cat on wheels. This version was propelled by the docile Latham supercharger.

I've created a monster! The owner, my buddy Jerry Lavoie, loved it and used it.

Not exactly a beauty, but it was effective. Olds powered rear engine roadster. Couldn't tell if it was coming or going.

A different approach. Ed Ruggeri and I built this oval racer to test our skills at our local track. Fortunately we had his dad Henry and his magnificent machine shop. Thank you Henry.

Ready and waiting to turn left!

'41 Ford with Landau top. I purchased this from Tino Valentine. I worked for Tino in his body shop for a short while. Soon after procurement I installed a Lincoln V12 in this lead bucket. The splash of lacquer is a reminder of my passion for its intoxicating aroma.

The Old, old Stroker gang—LA Roadster Show circa 2009. The Turk, Bob and Dan O'Connell, Jerry Lavoie, Bob, Rodger and Ralph Zepke. The essence of Hot Rodding.

On The Move

The Automotive Years - 1965 to 1980

Starting at the top — Chrysler Corporation

Magazine cover, first test at Irwindale California. Fun in the Sun, December 1967.

Perfect symmetrical lift, out of the box. Yours truly sans helmet. Not a good act—took some flak for this.

Just like new again. Completely restored, 1993.

Manufacturing setup at Hurst. The Dodge and Plymouth rollers, no engine, were dragged to the Detroit Hurst facilities by hook and wrecker. Here the future racer is being fitted with fiberglass front end. Final count 75 and 75.

No-fills Bostrom seats were fitted for driver and 'passenger'. Note the 'seatbelt' window pull in the center right.

Special cross member fitted to accept the Hemi into the 'A' Body with a minimum of trauma. Close proximity of the steering gear required a very special set of Headers.

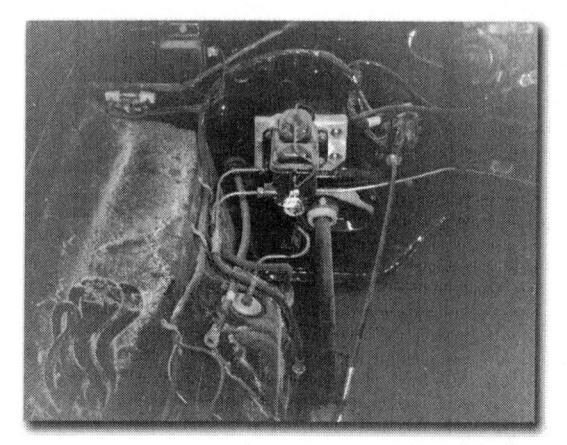

Special aluminum plate was required to shift the master cylinder outboard for cylinder head and rocker cover clearance.

A gentle massage was required on right shock tower to clear the right cylinder head and rocker cover.

Lastly, the proper axle setup was installed for either manual or automatic setup. In some cases the race teams showed up and loaded the parts and pieces before Hurst could fully assemble the vehicles. Time was of the essence.

Multitasking before computers. Chrysler crew servicing Bob Tullius at Marlboro 12-Hour. That's me as hood prop—pouring oil and removing headlight covers. BT won his class.

The Motley crew—**Hurst/NASCAR Dodge Dart.** Dan Mancini (Woodward Garage GM), Paul Phelps (Hemi Under Glass) and the Turk.

Tea Time Break. Paul and I in the wee hours at the Hurst facilities, during build-up of Dodge Dart.

Dan and Me. Dan Mancini, crew chief, crew and friend. And my helper Bobby T.

The Big time! Bristol, Darlington, Charlotte and here at Atlanta. A little pre-race conference between Paul and me.

And somehow it survived the season.

Off to Ray Nichols shop in Hammond, Indiana to build a **NASCAR,** DC-93. Why Not!

No photos of original test mule on the track. This is what it looked like at Daytona, minus the traffic.

Very early data acquisition. Yaw Meter. Base is attached to roof and rotates with vehicle. Shaft contains a slot (hidden) and rotates with the actual motion of the vehicle through the air.

thanks to Greg Kwiatkowski

Daytona September 1968, test mule #046. This was the first Dodge Charger 500. Forgive the quality of these images. They are all I have left of that small slice of history. If you remember, I was there, but I was somewhere else. Regrets, I have a few, and this is one of them.

Data acquisition at it's finest! Numerous sensors packaged to gather every nuance of the vehicle. With the size of this antiquated system it was good that we had a full size vehicle.

Getting ready. That spire protruding though the roof panel is the yaw meter. That's Larry the Laugher peeking at us from the left.

Garage shot. Ted MacAdow standing by the grille. I think that's me behind the steering wheel, but can't be sure.

Data pac brush recorder. Total chaos, but with a purpose. Now you can see why, years later, I almost had a disaster in the Trans Am with this very setup.

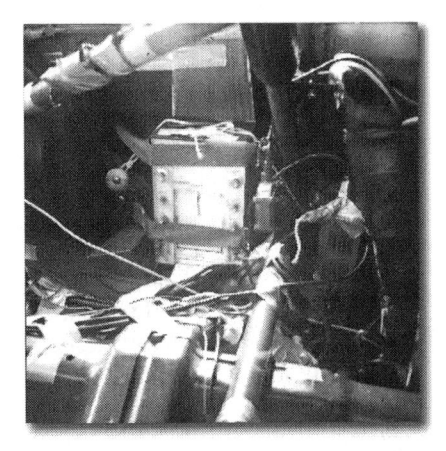

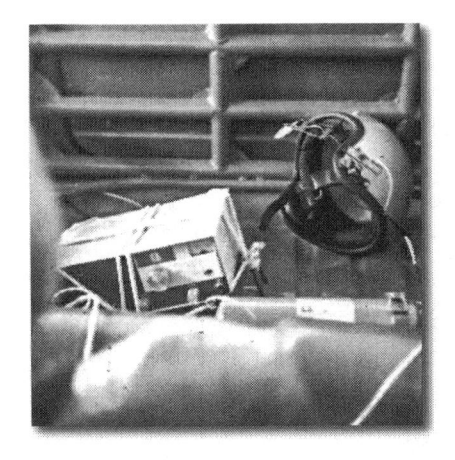

Early helmet communication development. Skull microphone setup. A little messy, but it worked.

Fast forward to DC-93 and its back to Detroit, a new nose job for entry, a wing for affect and a new life. That's Larry Rathgeb giving the driver some advice. Goodyear guys muling over the tires. Unknown character checking for mice in the fender bump.

All dressed up and ready for the prom.

What years of neglect can do! This corpse was found by Greg Kwiatkowski in the middle of no-where, beaten to a pulp. He plans a first class resurrection.

1968 Javelin. I surgically removed the McPherson strut and grafted on what I knew best. Upper and lower control arms and coil springs. From cerebral concepts, to paper, to metal. Just me, myself and I. Shear poetry.

My right hand, Paul Phelps. He welded and welded until we had to carefully extradite him from his self-captured cage.

Of course my ever faithful PITA (pain in the ass) bars follow me where ever I go. What do you think now Housebucket?

Two cars in the works. Primer version in the background was meant for yours truly. Faith stepped in. Tullius crashed and totaled the #1 car. #2 was pressed into service for Bob and I was regulated to the background, were I remained the rest of the season.

Bob was always a good listener, especially when it came to this new scene of turning left.

Neat custom dash, but it didn't make it go any faster! Sometimes you just can't help yourself.

Late night—they're always late nights. Just in time to get into some clean duds.

Getting some NASCAR award. Probably just for showing up? L-R Paul Phelps. the Turk and Bob Tullius.

The Hurst crew. R-L Sonny Blane, John Hutnick, Ed Ruggeri and Walt Czarnecki. I was prepping him for his future stint with Roger Penske.

The Turk, Bob Tullius, George Hurst and John Voelbel (AMC)

Daytona Road Course 1969, Paul Revere 250

Two very focused guys. Bob T and Bob T

The great carburettor caper. Saved by the hand of Ed U, a.k.a. Gary Condgon.

The Altercation ==>

The Fix ==>

The General is suppose to direct not get his hands dirty.

Moving on Again

The AAR Gang. Getting set for the kickoff.

AAR shop. Plymouth #1 on the fixture.

Based on correspondence and feedback from the website, I decided to include a series of build-up photos. They are far from complete. You need to remember that my main job was not photography. I was on the scene to point everybody in the right direction and my hands, eyes and ears were busy with this monumental task. It remains to be determined if I did an adequate j-o-b.

NASCAR type roll structure. Grab as much sheet metal as you can.

Horizontal shock towers. Connects axle to brackets to prevent rear wheel hop.

Looking forward under dash and at left door opening. Tie everything to brake and clutch brackets.

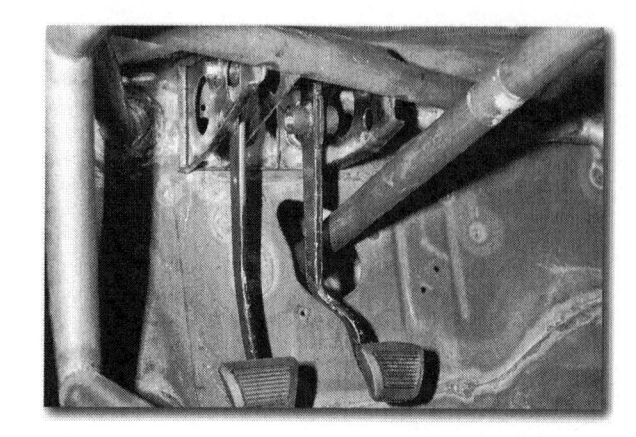

Pedal assembly. Brake setup for balance bar adjustable pivot to accommodate front to rear proportioning.

Engine compartment view. Note rollcage tie in. Lower left is the infamous 'pain in the ass bar'. These did not need to be removable.

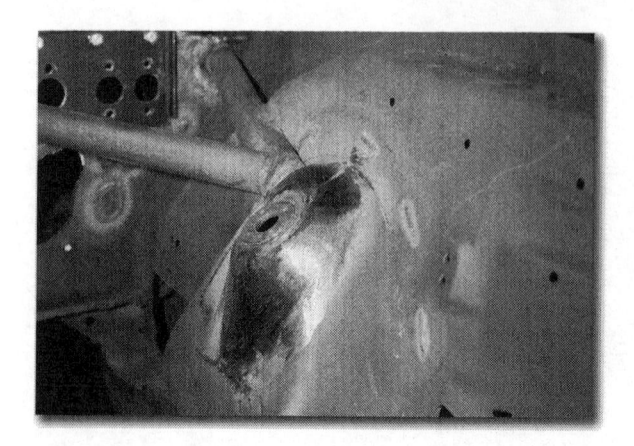

Shock tower bump-up for longer shocks. Again note the rollcage tie in.

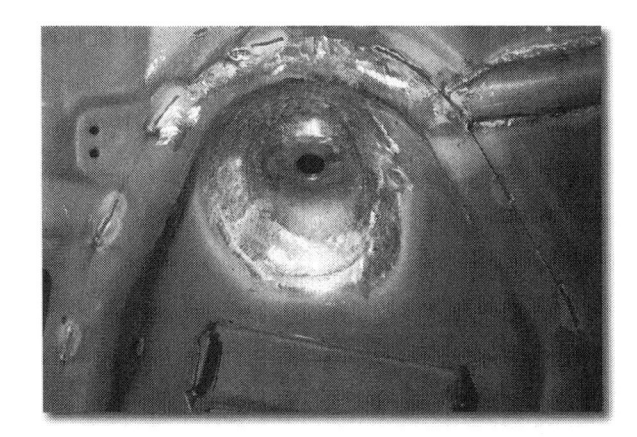

Underside of shock tower bump-up.

Front frame notches. Left notch for lower control arm. Front notch for LCA strut rod.

Titanium snake nest. Not for the faint of heart. Don't try this at home.

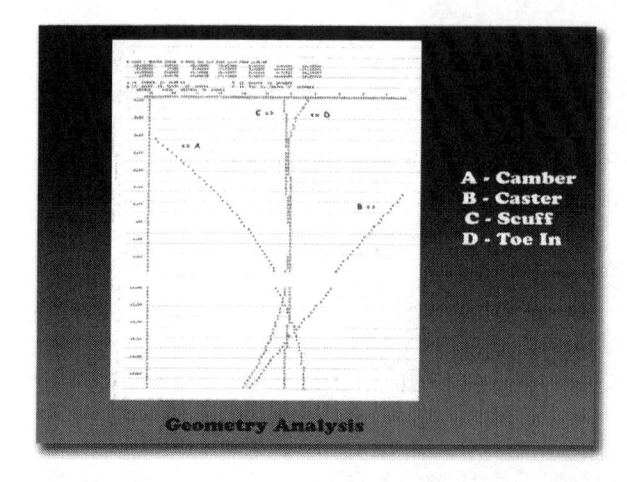

Computer study, such as it was, of race car geometry. Very little change from production. Toe pattern (bump steer) has to be dialed in.

A - Camber
B - Caster
C - Scuff
D - Toe In

Geometry Analysis

Upper control arm fixture to accommodate larger screw-in ball joint and angularity change.

Lower ball joint/ steering arm fixture to accommodate tie rod attachment point for toe pattern correction.

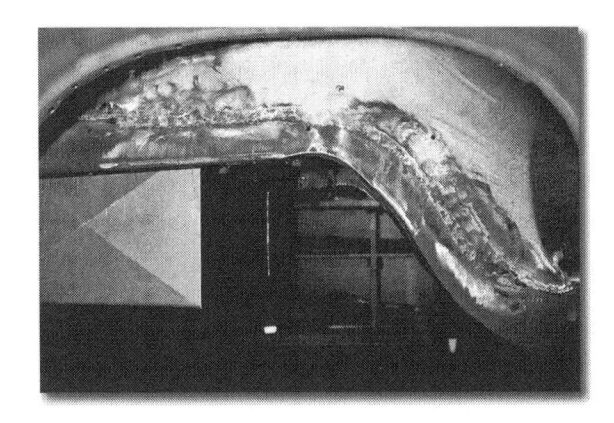

Rear frame notch for axle clearance. Also note frame reinforcement at kick-up. The rear box is fuel cell container.

Fender flare-out. Subtle, but necessary for tire clearance.

Quick-change radiator. Also note generous capacity for adequate cooling.

A few additional mods as I remember them.

'C' body torsion bar anchors (hex shaped receptacles) were installed in the lower control arms and at the T-bar anchor points in the rear cross member. This was to accommodate the larger NASCAR hex.

NASCAR front anti swaybar was installed onto the front cross member.

Rear anti swaybars were tried on several occasions, but were never found to be needed. We had adequate HP to induce oversteer when required.

A panhard rod was installed across the rear. One end attached to the frame and the other end attached to the axle. Reinforcement of the frame was necessary. Rod should be positioned so that the center of the rod coincides with center of the rear axle housing and is essentially horizontal. This is the approximate location of the 'roll center'. This does indeed result in a vertical movement of the roll center, which varies in left and right turns. Only the best of drivers will notice and they tend to accommodate. The P rod limits the lateral shift of the axle due to leaf spring deflection. Contrary to popular rumors we never did use a Watts Link.

Wheel hop was a constant problem. Our solution was to use a set of horizontal shock absorbers. Other linkages where tried but always resulted in 'fight' between the linkage and the leaf spring, and a violent oversteer.

Yes the cars were light enough to allow us to add lead shot in the rear frame horns. So be it.

Time To Hit The Road

Swede, I keep telling you time for your nails later.

Swede in action.

Dan, smooth as always.

My two main guys, Bobby Box and Bert Brown fussing over a 'pissy' lug nut.

The BOSS at work, directing traffic, Road America.

The way it should have always been.

The Nerd and The Beauty, St. Jovite Canada.

A bon farewell from all the gang.

All is new again. Fully restored AAR 'Cuda. #42 fresh out of the shop, ready to run again at Sonoma, CA. This was the #1 vehicle, originally #48, got it's numbers changed to #42 at Saint Jovite where it remained until years end.

Next Stop Southgate California.

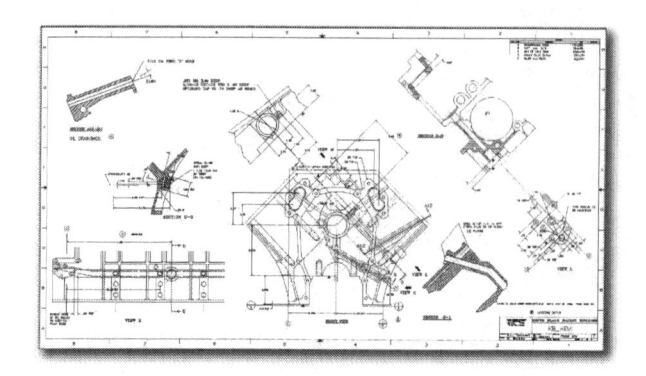

The start of it all. Paper drawing of the Keith Black aluminum Top Fuel block.

Block #1 stayed on the stand until KB found his brave with the help of Candies & Hughes.

The best way to keep it all contained. Y-block and side bolted main caps.

202

My Diploma from Keith Black

The Designer

The designer sat at his drafting board,
A wealth of knowledge in his head was stored.
Like what can be done on a radial drill,
Or a turret lathe or a vertical mill?
But above all things a knack he had,
For driving gentle machinists mad.
So he mused as he thoughtfully scratched his bean,
Just how can I make this thing hard to machine?
If I make this perfect body straight,
The job had ought to come out first rate.
But it would be so easy to turn and bore,
That it would never make the machinist sore.
So I'll put a compound taper there,
And a couple of angles to make them swear.
And brass would work for this little gear,
But it's too damned easy to work I fear.
So just to make the machinist squeal,
I'll have him mill it from tungsten steel.
And I'll put these holes that hold the cap,
Down underneath where they can't be tapped.
Now if they can make this, it'll just be luck,
Cause it can't be held by dog or chuck,
And it can't be planed and it can't be ground,
So I feel my design is unusually sound.
Then he shouted with glee, "Success at last!
This goddam thing can't even be cast!"

The acid test as it were, Irwindale, California. The timex meets the asphalt. Long range shot but that's me on the right of the white ambulance in a white Tee shirt. I wanted to be up close to the action. Not concerned about loose pieces. The ultimate confidence.

Mike Snively cool as ever and straight as an arrow. Just another day at the ball park, except for Keith.

Reunited after all those years. Restored to perfection. Las Vegas, Mopar's on the Strip, 2013.

First attempt at making an aluminum version Street Hemi. Water leaks plagued us from day one. Multi configured composition gasket got us up and running.

The every versatile Mike Snively playing with his pipes in the background.

Keith Black dyno console. Getting setup for the 305 NASCAR lunch box test to simulate the Daytona 500.

Mario Rossi prepares to install 305 in his winged Dodge at Daytona 1971.

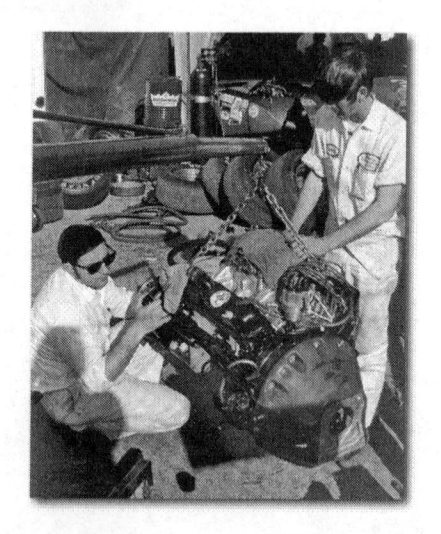

Dick Brooks #22. Started the 1971 Daytona 500 in 8th. Lead for a total of five laps and finished 7th after a crash with Pete Hamilton.

Preparation for 1971 Questor Grand Prix at Ontario Motor Speedway. Formula One & Formula A Invitational. An Eagle nestled among the blocks and cranks at KBRE.

Swede Savage received the invitation, Bruce Junor and I provided the car and engine, along with the 'expertise'.

Competition was fierce. Car ran in the middle of the pack until failed throttle caused a crash. Awesome experience, unimpressive performance.

Pit stop conference. Jim Wright looking over Swedes shoulder, the Turk looking cool, and Mike Mills adding encouragement.

Looked like we belonged, but alas everything was so rushed it turned out poorly. Lesson learned.

Before the detour into the track barrier, the best we mustered was 25th. Not quite where we wanted to be.

One of the many other side jobs I had. Supervised all off-road racing, Bill Stroppe, Walker Evans and John Baker. Here I am riding shotgun with John Baker in the Las Vegas offroad extravaganza.

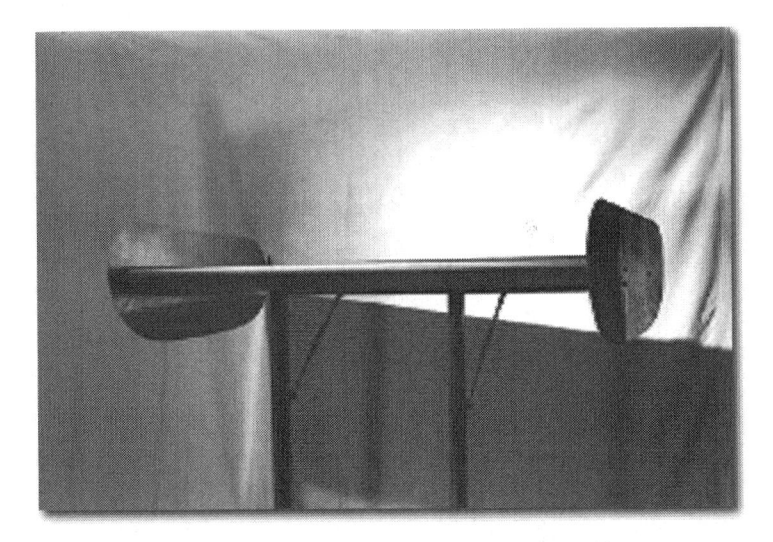

Again one my 'side' jobs for KB. He talked me into designing and building this wing for Don Garlits, circa 1973. DG insisted on installing it himself. Bad deal. Not enough support and it flew as not intended. Put him off of wings for a while, but he later had to get back on the band wagon.

Noise abatement 101. Our attempt at controlling the noise level while not effecting power output. It worked!

Pollution, what pollution?

Number one crank-trigger setup. I did the mechanical stuff and Ron Killen flew in to tweak the electronics.

Accolades From A Friend

PATRICK BEDARD

• Bob Tarozzi is still on his first vodka martini. We haven't even ordered dinner yet. But already he is leading us through the back doors of the unique Southern California speed business.

"I guess there is no need for it to be a secret anymore," he allows in the casual tone that can be used in discussing old achievements. "We've seen 800 horsepower out of the Hemi."

"Alcohol?" I say, trying my very best to sound unimpressed.

"No. Gas."

"Gasoline?"

"Yeah . . . and carburetors."

Across the table, Don Sherman hunches forward over his vermouth, incredulous, like he'd just seen God . . . who was wearing an Isky T-shirt at the time. John Eberhart, whose mental processes were forever altered by an L88-powered '57 Chevy he built as a youth, is in rapture. For myself, it's like hearing that a cancer cure has been OKed by the Food and Drug Administration.

When I left Chrysler Engineering six years ago, they were turning the Hemi to 6500 rpm, grossing 530 horsepower and congratulating themselves all the way to Six Mile Road. Two years ago they had worried it up another hundred horsepower and reckoned they were at the end of the line.

"That's stroked to 477," Tarozzi admits, "but a 426 will give you 730. And the drag racers run those to 9000."

The thought of pistons the size of flower pots moving that fast is too much to contemplate over an empty glass. We are forced to order another round.

Tarozzi talks the life of an adventurer roving the horsepower arena. And he looks the part; Blackbeard shined up and slipped into a sport jacket. But in fact, he is a mechanical engineer with closetful of degrees and a record of resourcefulness, sometimes to excess. He admits to having been kicked out of his local drag strip more than once as a kid for using an illegal oxygen injection system ("it worked but you could melt the motor pretty easy"). And a search of the records would probably show that he has hit the wall at Darlington more times during a single race ("mostly in practice; I did OK in the race . . . until right near the end") than anyone else. Maybe that is why he canceled out on the driving and re-emerged in 1970 as the Crew Chief on Dan Gurney's team of Trans-Am Barracudas.

Now he is a freelance engineer specializing in engine development. His proving ground is a dyno cell at Keith Black's shop in Southgate, California. His clients include Chrysler (drag race development on the Hemi), Keith Black (design of an aluminum Hemi block) and anybody else who has an engine problem and money ("some boat racer wants me to design an aluminum overhead-cam head for the Slant Six"). All of this gives him very much an insider's view of the racing engine business. It's a high-speed life and he speaks of it with gusto, whether he is describing failures in double-purple valve springs or roundly denouncing the management at some company that contracts him.

The waitress brings a tray of shooters and we get serious about this 800 hp Hemi.

"Carburetors are better than timed fuel injection," he says.

> ❝ Avarice and overkill in the Dyno Room, the amazing Multi Strike, king-hell carburetors, crankcase explosion. Waitress, another shooter for my friend ❞

"What? How can that be!"

"The vaporizing fuel cools the intake charge better so you get more power. The only thing wrong with carburetors is that we can't get Holley to tool up one big enough."

It sounds like heresy. But he should know. Over the salad we hear about the latest in Camshaft Science, a discipline bordering on outright witchcraft.

"Would you believe we're using 0.750 inches of net lift at the valve now?" he asks, knowing full well that I won't, knowing that if I didn't know about carburetors I'm hopelessly out of date and he can manipulate me up pushrods and down oil galleries for the rest of the night.

"Gosh, Mr. Wizard, that's twice the lift of a stock cam. The last I heard, the racers were struggling with 0.600 and the accelerations were so great the heads were being snapped off the valves. You must be getting some very sophisticated lobes."

(CONTINUED)

PATRICK BEDARD (CONTINUED)

"Yep. Multiple polynomial curves. There are only maybe three cam grinders—and probably General Motors—that understand them. Nobody on the West Coast."

Dinner arrives. Something about his Alaska King Crab legs must remind him of connecting rods. We peel off into a fourth-power analysis, complete with footnotes and dyno readings, of the Long Rod vs. Short Rod controversy. He concludes that short rods produce more torque, which makes them *better* for road racing—contrary to the prevailing popular opinion, at least when last I heard . . . which was about twenty minutes before dinner.

My salmon is excellent. I'm trying to concentrate on the flavor. Sherman has almost finished his halibut or whatever it was. Tarozzi remembers the Multi Strike.

"The what?"

"Trick new double-throw-down ignition system. Invented by a guy from Chrysler Aerospace. It'll make that 0.750-lift Hemi idle right down to 800 rpm."

I forget the salmon; Sherman ignores his halibut. We have to know about Multi Strike.

"Makes more than one spark. Keeps making them for twenty crankshaft degrees. Above 7000 rpm there is only enough time for maybe two sparks, but at idle you can get up to twenty. So it can fire off rich mixtures . . . cover up bad fuel distribution."

It sounds like magic—*more* magic, I should say. I have no mind for electronics. What I need is coffee. How about an after-dinner shot? Tarozzi orders something nobody including the waitress ever heard of; settles for Lochan Ora. I want whisky. Sherman and Eberhart pass. They don't want to numb their sensors and miss the next round of wonderment. Tarozzi slides into the latest schemes of the West Coast cam grinders.

"They're doing Energy Crisis cams," he laughs. "Low lift and low duration. And no power. One of the guys in the shop has one in his pick-up. Last weekend he threw a couple of dirt bikes in the back and headed up over the Grapevine toward Bakersfield. Had to hold it right to the wood on the hills. Peaks out at seventy on the flat."

"You mean these cam guys think people are going to want to change cams to get better gas mileage?"

"That's nothing. Engle is making 4-cylinder engines out of V-8s. Takes out half the pistons. Puts bob weights on the crank. Makes dummy tappets for the deactivated cylinders so the valves don't open."

Sherman is laughing so hard he almost slides under the table.

"He screwed up the first one. Didn't allow for expansion in the pushrods. So the intake valves opened about five thousandths and let gas run down into the oil. Next time he started it the crankcase exploded. Blew up the oil pan."

The waitress comes by and asks if we want the check. No. Tarozzi is just warming to his subject. What we really need is another round of shooters to clear our minds. •

CAR and DRIVER

Baseline dyno setup with deep wet sump oil pan. Oil level set high so that no power losses occurred due to windage.

IR (Individual Runner) manifold to mimic Fuel Injection, except it was better, until one faithful day in the life of the 305!

Intake runner length evaluation. Up and down and then up again. FI throttle body to simplify fuel loads.

Dry sump aplenty. Looks like eight stages of suction. Haven't gone to the −16 lines quite yet. Careful what you wish for, you might get it and then find you can't use it.

One of many, many oil pans. Generally speaking you just need a lot of suckers.

Base pump configuration below. Pressure section on the right and add as many suction stages as you can tolerate. I never found the limit.

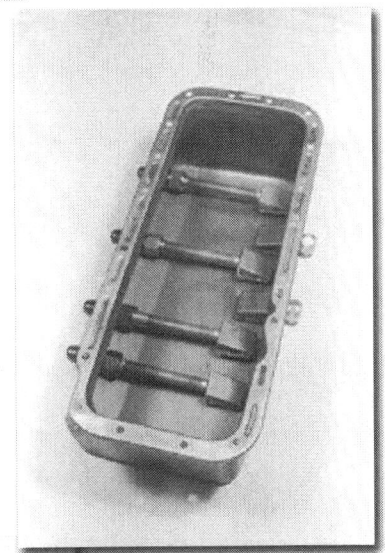

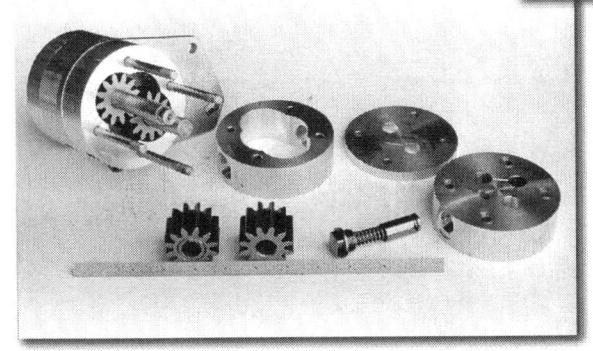

Once the oil pan was made we would evaluate depth to the crank by inserting various spacers. Here you see a four inch spacer.

We didn't forget the 440's. Here is a hand fabricated large-plenum manifold. Fuel distribution was a nightmare. Popsicle sticks galore.

Now here's what it takes to be a real dyno operator. You see, you hear, but most of all you feel. Slight change in vibrations in the floor 'told' me to shut the throttle, and I did! One-eight from the edge.

Moving North

New digs. **Don Nichols and his UOP** operation moved to Marina, CA and I inherited these really upscale digs. For awhile anyways.

First cut at a turbo package for the slant six. All hand built manifolds made from sheet steel.

Slant six package ready to go into a pickup. Tom Hoover showed up, drove for a few miles, then headed east to Detroit. Now that's a supreme show of confidence. Thanks for everythingTom!

318 V8 package. Shipped to Ted Spehar at Special Vehicles in Detroit and popped into a van. It got lots of play time.

Four cylinder Mitsubishi also shipped back to Special Vehicles to be installed in a wee car of some sort. No complaints.

Now to the serious stuff. Old faithful 305 all dressed up for Formula A/5000. UOP Shadow converted from their Chevy power to this version of the Dodge. Quite successfully I might add. Kinsler FI and a multistage dry sump.

Forced to do a little thinking. I changed from my engine hat to chassis hat and was sorting the handling shortcomings.

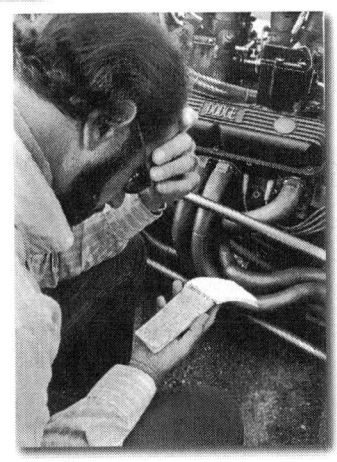

SCCA attempted to change CanAm to 305 engines. UOP grafted fenders onto the F5000. Instant Can-Am. Alan Jones came over to test drive at Riverside. That's me in the bearded disguise.

The After Years — 1980 to 2013

The 80s

The 80s were, in a sense a lost generation, I produced no offsprings. However I must admit that without this time and without this place I would have amounted to absolutely nothing in a financial sense. I have alluded to the fact that racing, even as involved as I was, pays nothing. You work for pittance and you endure that sort of short-sheeting on a 24/7 basis. So my detour into the depths of litigation was a necessary one that then allowed me to return to my natural habitat the race biz.

There are things that we are meant to do, make that destined to do, and for me it was the act of creating, producing and driving very fast and quick land vehicles. They may have been able to survive without me, but I could never have survived without them, one and all. Now I suppose I sound like a demented old man. Au contraire, I am extremely fortunate in that I was from a time and place when individualism was a positive and meaning pursuit. Where an individual was able to pursue a course of his liking, and wear a multitude of hats and faces. And I was there, damn it, I was there. Nothing is forever and I am eternally grateful that I was able to accomplished all that I have and look back with a gleam in my eye —you did good Turk, you did good.

When the phone rings, what do you do. You should all know by now—you answer it!

Whooeee now this is the big time, LeMans —France that is.

The welcome sign is out for the blokes from the U.S of A.

Where's Waldo? I'll save you the time. Just follow the little gray arrow.

Bob Tullius performing his assigned task. Strategically placing the decals. He would occasionally take a turn at the wheel and perform his stab and steer routine.

Lanky Foushee. Little can be said of guy who could do it all, and at the end of the day put you on the deck with his humor from the hills.

Brian Krem. Master of engines and extremely adroit at wielding a ten pound hammer for maximum effect.

There he is, Waldo again, slinking in the shadows. Beware, he is about to commit an extremely brutal act.

The fateful scene. About to destroy a camshaft to 'improve' the performance. All the guilty parties are skillfully hidden from prying camera lenses. Now we need to wait for the appropriate moment.

The appropriate moment— we thought. Man plans, God laughs!

Because of our poor timing, and exceptional performance from the now eleven cylinder engine, Bob scooted past the start/finish line before the 24 hour mark. Requiring yet another lap under painfully concerning conditions.

The fans attacked the track in unprecedented frenzy—requiring a revision of the finish line. After the first two finishers, the remainder of the race cars were stopped just short of the official finish line and shuttled directly into parc ferme, just around the corner.

Yeah, right down there in the parc ferme under temporary lockdown. Sometimes the good guys get a break.

Home at last, home at last!

"Well Lanky whatsya think?" "I'm all thunk out Turk, I'm all thunk out."

A very worried man was Brian Krem. Just hoping and praying nobody caught him on camera with hammer in flight.

Na, Turk says you did good Brian, you did good.

Bangladesh in the dry.

Bangladesh in the wet. Not much difference, you still can't get around.

The smiling Bang man. He thinks he has the solution. I think not.

It all started like this. Bill Jennings and John Hutnick put together a slick concept. Clay model shows some elegance.

I stepped in and created a simple chassis and suspension.

Then added a little power with train to match. It worked but didn't 'fly'.

226

The Talons get a grip on the asphalt. Paul Rossi's multi-car team in IMSA road racing. Took advantage of my 'talents' when I could break away from my other diversions.

I'm listening to race comm, my daughter Kristine is tuned into a much different channel.

Paul and an array of helpers and drivers. Me, I'm just showing off my new pink hat, styling.

Mitsubishi Stealth. Getting ready for a mighty attempt at the daunting Pikes Peak.

Alan Junor, my goto guy on the Feuling/Menard Indy project, got involved in prepping a **Wienermobile**. It seemed that they found the steering and braking connections outside and in front of the hotdog, oops.

A couple of days, a few magical revisions, a little witchcraft and we had a usable vehicle.

The steering and braking neatly tucked behind the 200 mph bumper.

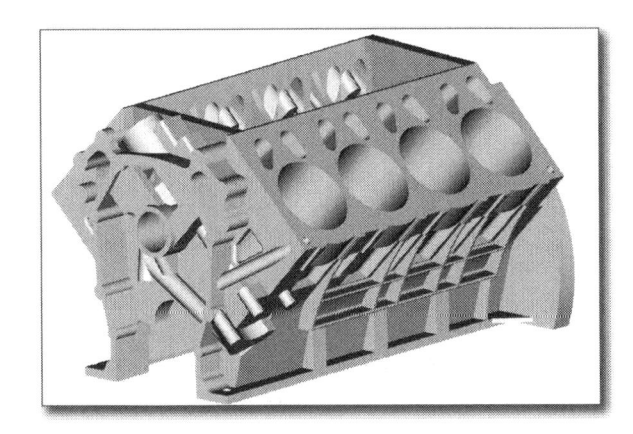

Not just a pretty picture. A CAD solid model of BAE's entry into the cast aluminum Hemi top fuel engine block market. A new look for a sustainable product.

The forged version with a little magic from the wizardry of CNC. Gone are the side ribbing, now decorative, but necessary in the land of castings. I miss them, but what the hell that's progress.

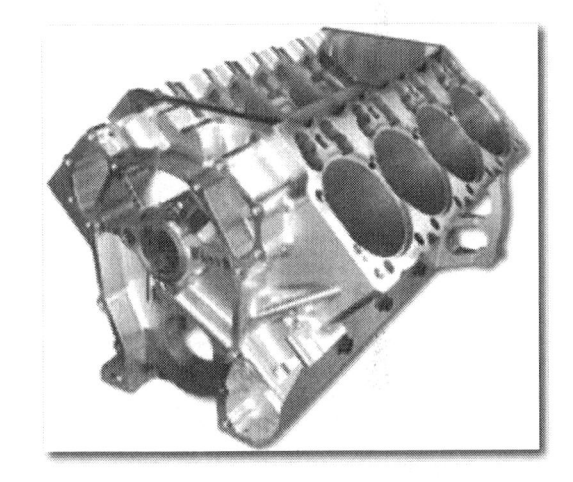

Shelly Anderson putting her dads products to the test.

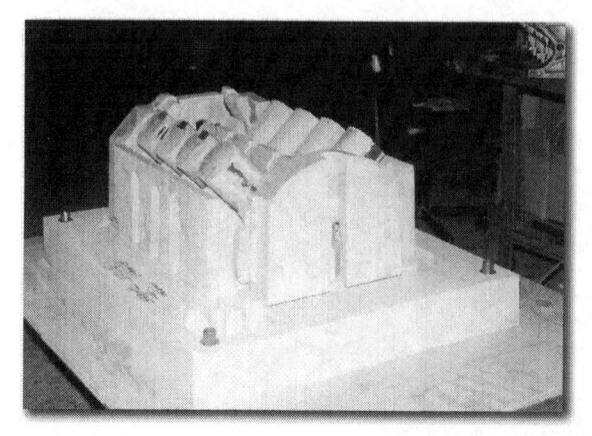

A little insight into the casting process. You're looking at the lower portion of the mold. These bits and pieces, cores, are formed with pepset resin sand. It cures to full hardness in minutes at room temperature.

The upper portion of the mold, complete with its requisite cores, is lowered onto the lower portion.

And now we pour the molten aluminum into the sealed mold. Careful it's hot!

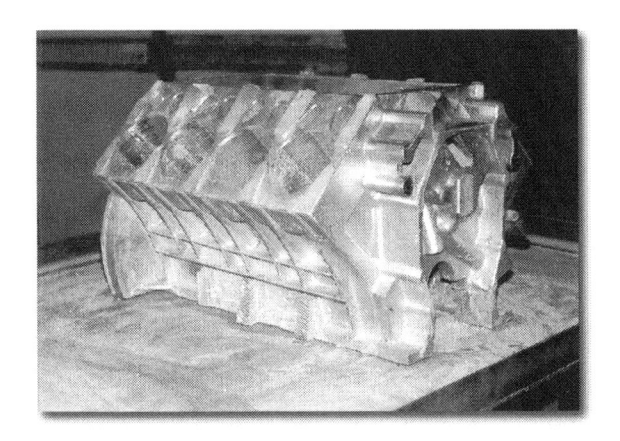

The completed casting, cleaned up a bit. The total pour is about twice the amount of metal you retain. Careful inspection is required at this point to detect defects. Aircraft quality would dictate X-rays, but for the lowly drag racer, what you see is what you get.

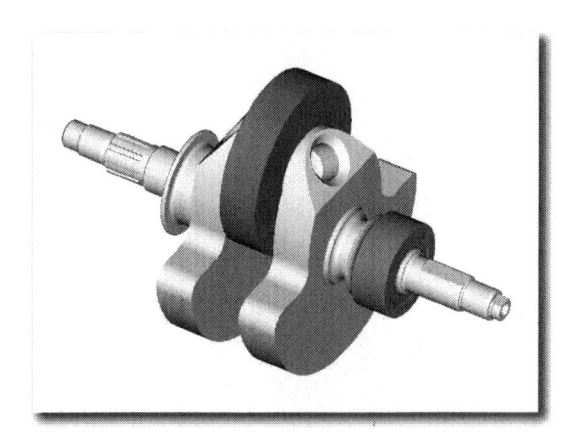

Harley Davidson one-piece crankshaft. Dark grey rounds are simulated components for balance sorting. Simple, and anticipated to be cheaper, but HD had a serious aversion to change.

Link rod. Originally called a slave rod, but offended the politically correct persons at HD. Well excuuuuse me!

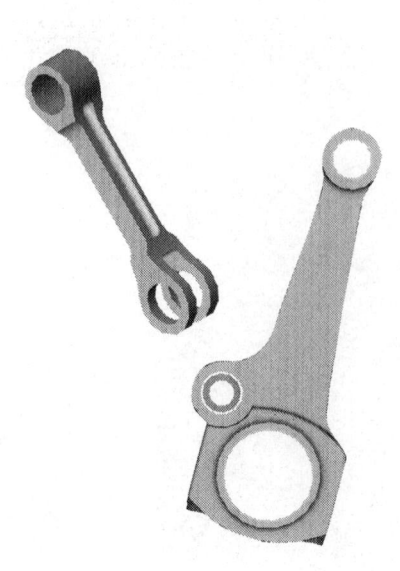

Master rod. This arrangement required because of the in-line configuration of the HD cylinder banks.

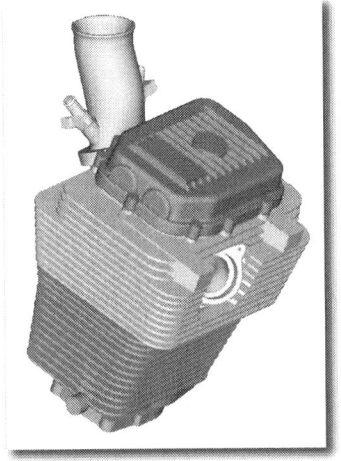

Harley-Beull engine reconfigured for attempt at AMA class racing. The benefits of CAD modeling. You start with one—

and quickly and effortlessly make a twin brother, complete with fuel injection.

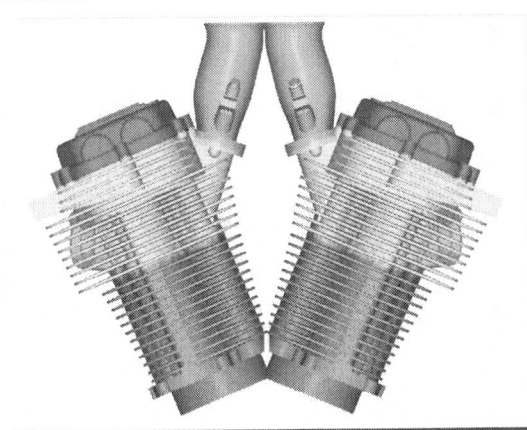

A few months, it was bolted up to the dyno and made lots of noise.

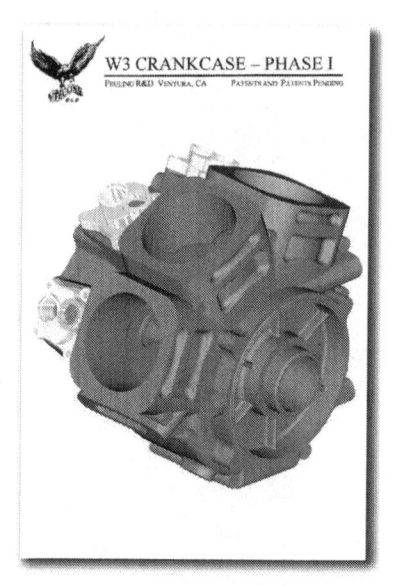

A crap-shoot that went south. A **W3 twin cam**. Added a third cylinder to the existing casting and formed up a connecting rod with two extra lugs to accommodate the additional two links.

More than just a pretty picture. Stress analysis of the W3 connecting rod under simulated stress.

New extended wheelbase frame to accommodate the extra cylinder.

Rest the brain and work the body. Time off as it were. My competitive obsession got me off on a tangent that few believe. Started slow and easy and then went flat out, pedal to the metal.

One of my really favorite events—Criterium's. Elbow to elbow competition on two skinny assed tires and just a set of skivvies to cover your butt.

Probably one of the few times in my life that I followed the line.

The main event—**The Kona Ironman.**

A refreshing swim out and back for a total of 2.5 miles.

A causal bicycle ride around the beautiful island of Hawaii, for 112 miles.

Then move those two little feet for a total of 26.2 miles and just get home before dark. Piece of cake.

Engine Corporation of America (ECA). A complete electric generation package destined to supply electricity to remote villages in third world countries. Generators were to be attached to the four ends of the twin cranks.

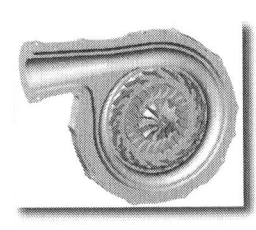

Special water cooled turbocharger required to generate extremely high pressure to produce high outputs at very high efficiencies.

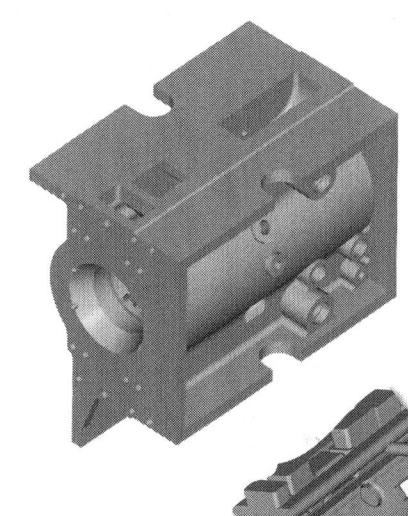

Inner water core, below, will be subtracted from the main block, left, to produce finished block with air, water and oil

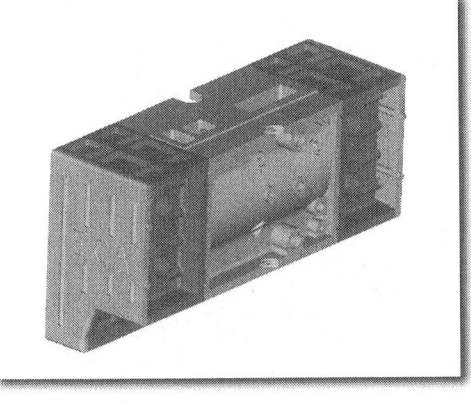

Completed assembly. Block, crankcase halves and end caps.

Master inventor Dr. Marius Paul standing proud next to his creation. The electric generators fit into the round cup like protrusions. Four in all.

Now we have the Turk standing next to the finished monster, sort of Frankenstein like.

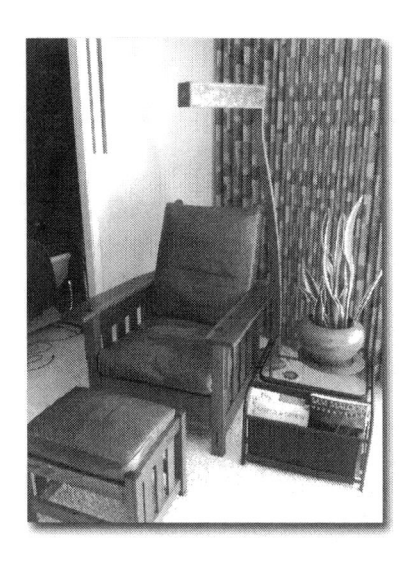

Because my creative energies went unattended, I sat down in front of my computer once again and from various hand sketches generated these functional beauties.

My hands were useful once again. No longer immersed in grease, just lightly dusted.

Spent months in the shop with planks of reclaimed chestnut from West Virginia, complete with worm holes and nail voids.

By chance I located an original California chestnut tree rescued from old Sacramento, California to create my entry door.

A cherry wood Morris chair redesigned to minimize its overbearing masculine features, and complemented with the delicate marquetry figures.

240

Finally I'm where I belong and always shoulda been!

Track and sky. I love the sweet smell of Castrol in the morning, it smells like victory.

I wish I didn't know now, what I didn't know then!

Rossi   Biaggi   Schettino

Still trying after all these years!

Tarozzi

On the podium, sort of. Mustered to attention by my good friend Steve Stanley.

Turn 5 at Laguna Seca. The Turk vs Casey Stoner. Separated by 50 years and about 30 mph.

After fifty years we're still together and going to hit the road again! Never a truer love.

That crazy gal of mine had enough trust and faith in me to get on the back of that crotch rocket, motor down the length of California Hwy 1 to Big Sur and yonder. Love her beyond words.

On the road.
Route 66

The Grand Canyon one of a number of random stops, aside from the requisite diner break at Goldie's Diner in Williams Arizona.

The road goes on forever, but I must head for home.

the dreams have faded
never to glow again
the memories have scattered
never to be mustered again
the fun has dissipated
never to be as it was

and the Turk has left the building

nothing happens without risk

GUY CLARK
"The Cape"

Eight years old with a flour sack cape tied all around his neck
He climbed up on the garage, he's figurin' what the heck, well
He screwed his courage up so tight that the whole thing come unwound
He got a runnin' start and bless his heart, he's headed for the ground

Well, he's one of those who knows that life is just a leap of faith
Spread your arms and hold your breath and always trust your cape

Now, he's all grown up with a flour sack cape tied all around his dream
And he's full of spit and vinegar and he's bustin' at the seam
Well, he licked his finger and he checked the wind, it's gonna be do or die
And he wasn't scared of nothin', boys, he was pretty sure he could fly

Well, he's one of those who knows that life is just a leap of faith
Spread your arms and hold your breath and always trust your cape

Now, he's old and gray with a flour sack cape tied all around his head
And he's still jumpin' off the garage and will be till he's dead
All these years the people said, he was actin' like a kid
He did not know he could not fly and so he did

Well, he's one of those who knows that life is just a leap of faith
Spread your arms and hold your breath and always trust your cape
Yes, he's one of those who knows that life is just a leap of faith
Spread your arms and hold your breath and always trust your cape

Made in the USA
Charleston, SC
22 January 2016